POTENTIAL
*The Way to Emotional Maturity*

# POTENTIAL

## *The Way to*
## *Emotional Maturity*

# HUGH DOWNS

1973

*Doubleday & Company, Inc., Garden City, New York*

ISBN: 0-385-03742-2
Library of Congress Catalog Card Number 72-96235
Copyright © 1973 by Hugh Downs
Printed in the United States of America
First Edition

*This book is dedicated to Sadim Young,*
*who at age three has a chance.*

# FOREWORD

This book comprises an informal discussion of the concept of maturity in the human individual. In general it is an attempt to show that "maturity," a word so much used but so frequently only vaguely understood, is capable of practical and useful definition; to discuss why and how maturity is a desirable condition; to demonstrate that maturity is an attainable state, and to show avenues by which it might be reached by any of us.

Most of the more formal definitions of the concept of maturity are, logically, the definitions of psychologists, as also the majority of published material on the value and attainment of maturity is by psychologists. But it is my contention that the answers we seek cannot come out of the science of psychology alone. Among other things, the evolution of the concept of maturity must be examined, and this in turn involves ethical judgments and assumed goals.

In the book I am inviting the reader to consider with me this evolution of the concept, and the various definitions of the idea of maturity that we employ today; to explore with me the links between maturity and happiness; and finally to consider practical means for achieving in our own lives that which we mean by maturity.

Obviously we are concerned here with *motivation* of individuals, and inevitably the book will be categorized as "self-help"—which brings up an interesting dilemma, mainly semantical. In a case like this, an invitation or exhortation to "be motivated" is redundant, since anyone interested in "self-help" is already motivated. Moreover, any help that comes from outside is not really *self*-help.

But in spite of the paradox, in spite of the fact that no treatise —or no friend, psychiatrist, priest, counselor, or whatever—can produce volition in another person, as a practical matter there are demonstrable links between counseling and what we call self-help. They lie in such things as the study of philosophies that offer practical plans for adherents to follow, in the evaluation of case histories of psychiatric success, and in the rarer fact of inspiration to change by sometimes indefinable emotional reaction to outside influence. As we shall see, some of the definitions of maturity take cognizance of these links and attempt to explain them, at the same time pointing up inadequacies of the purely scientific approach to understanding and attaining maturity; and certain fallacies in Western thought in general. This latter point bears with it the necessity of considering dangers inherent in the blanket acceptance of alternatives to Western philosophies, such as the mysticism of certain systems of Eastern thought, and introduces the need for caution.

What emerges in this discussion is the connection between the value of individual maturity and evolutionary goals involving social maturity. And although the goals and the precise paths to such goals may be as yet obscure, the direction is clear. We are talking about an ideal world for the individual and for humanity— for men and for Man.

Finally, it goes without saying that the author is not speaking herein from a pinnacle of professional authority, nor indeed even from a plateau of personally attained maturity. I repeat that this is a purely informal presentation, and I hope the reader will share my interest in exploring the questions and the answers, and recognize that my own interest stems as much from want as from achievement.

Hugh Downs

# CONTENTS

POTENTIAL
*The Way to Emotional Maturity*

# CHAPTER I

## Getting It Together

[1]

Logically, one starts with a definition.

In the consideration of the concept of "maturity," however, one of the reasons it is a word more widely used than understood is not a dearth of definition, but the contrary. For maturity comprises many aspects and is ascribed many definitions. Before we examine some of the latter generalities, I think it will be useful to begin by looking at one specific aspect of maturity—a familiar phenomenon we shall call by a currently popular phrase.

"Getting it together," in counterculture parlance, implies that it is at the moment all apart. It suggests a condition of personal fragmentation, and a need to unify inwardly.

How often have we sensed in ourselves conflicting drives, inconsistent goals, ambivalent desires? A mild schizophrenic outlook with regard to what we think we want? It is as though we operate at times from diverse or multiple centers of being, centers not in touch with each other but capable of alternately dominating our waking life.

Did you ever, late at night, suspend work on a project in order to get some sleep, determined to bound out of bed the following morning early, certain you would resume your enthusiasm—only to decide when the alarm rang that another hour or two in bed was more important?

Did you ever awaken with a smoked-out, soot-lined throat, and promise yourself to give up smoking as of that instant, marveling at the ease of your decision and the firmness of your resolve—only to find that by noon or earlier nothing would better suit your well-being than a cigarette?

Did you ever quit drinking for good because of a hangover, and then start again the same day, your disgust and resolution both having evaporated as your health and thirst returned?

Make your own list, from compulsive sex encounters alternating with remorse, the dessert table vs. the new crash diet, the collisions between asceticism and hedonism, security and challenge, struggle and surrender.

There is nothing grossly abnormal about feeling different at different times. Alternation of appetite and satiety is one of the rhythms of life and can be enjoyed at either node. But it is evidence of not "having it together" to be so affected by a given phase of "reformation" that sudden and excessive promises result.

One can choose to quit smoking or drinking or philandering or malingering or gluttonizing, and really strive for the goal all throughout varying feelings and conditions; or one can continue to smoke and drink and goof off and gamble and squander and gorge and drift and drop out—without in either case manifesting the kind of immaturity that might be called the Jekyll-and-Hyde trap. Dr. Jekyll became Mr. Hyde, you remember, through chemistry. And it is possible that all our moods and aspects are controlled by or at least related to chemistry—either simple ingested chemicals or subtle self-generated biochemicals or toxins created by invading micro-organisms and the antitoxins we create to neutralize them.

The feeling of needing to "get it together" is the feeling that we are operating from different centers of being at different times. It is the knowledge that we can't make and hold to meaningful plans unless we become more inwardly unified. The feeling of disunity in turn comes from short-term identity of self with a chemical condition and mood of the moment. The knowledge that we either compulsively struggle or passively permit ourselves to be buffeted about by the flux of our internal chemistry creates a thirst for an identity center that *endures*. This is the thirst for maturity.

The more mature person, though he may be fully aware of differing moods, will not be victimized by them. He may suffer a hangover (although he is much less likely to do so) but he will not make promises he can't keep, and he will know that all things pass. He will base his resolves on averaged-out attitudes and self-determined goals. His opinion will be, literally, a considered one. His emotions will be felt and appropriately expressed, but he will not be tossed about by them. He will have it all together.

This is only one aspect of maturity. From an orthodox psychological standpoint it relates to cohesiveness and integration of personality facets. In the larger context of maturing it provides the kind of base that allows for detachment and the growth of self-actualization.

Now let us go on to other aspects, other definitions.

[2]

Long lists of experts have stressed the fact that love is the main characteristic of normalcy and health. In this sense the ability to love means simply the ability to give unconditional love. Fromm and Fromme, Reik and Reich, along with other popularizers, have written whole books on the subject, the gist of which is that the ability to love is characteristic of the mature person.

Freud said that a normal person "should be able to *love* and *work*." Other physicians would add "play" to these two activities. Still another, Richard Cabot, in his book *What Men Live By*,* listed love, work, play, and worship as the activities a healthy person lives by. Whether our lists be limited or long, "our choice is

* Boston: Houghton Mifflin, 1914.

based," Cabot contends, "on ethical grounds, and not on scientific fact."

The contention is corroborated by the more detailed criteria of maturity offered by psychologists, for example, "character and integrity in the ethical sense." F. Barron adds "effective organization or work toward goals," "correct perception of reality," and "interpersonal and intrapersonal adjustment."† A. H. Maslow, in *Motivation and Personality*, lists these attributes: more comfortable relations with reality; acceptance of self, others, and nature; spontaneity; problem centering; detachment (in the need for privacy and in the sense that friendships and attachments to family not be of the "clinging, intrusive and possessive variety"); independence of culture and environment; continued freshness of appreciation; limitless horizons; social feeling; deep but selective social relationships; democratic character structure ("respect [for] any human being just because he is a human individual"); ethical certainty; unhostile sense of humor; and creativeness.

Moving still farther afield, we find characteristics of maturity accepted by orthodox psychology that overlap with some Eastern concepts, in that they deal with ideas of self and ego pondered in Hindu and Buddhist thought centuries ago. Among these are extension of the sense of self, the connection between humor and piety,‡ the fictional character of ego, and generic conscience (as differing from the child's obedience to "must," which is a conscience stemming from specific commandments handed down from tribe or family). The generic conscience is self-actualizing: It

† "Personal Soundness in University Graduate Students," *Publications in Personality Assessment and Research*, No. 1. Berkeley: University of California Press, 1954.

‡ Gordon Allport writes, "It may help to understand the religious sentiment . . . if we compare it with humor. In one respect only are they alike. Both set a worrisome event in a new frame of reference, smashing, as it were, the context of literal-mindedness. Both humor and religion shed new light on life's troubles by taking them out of the routine frame. To view our problems humorously is to see them as of little consequence, to view them religiously is to see them in a serious scheme of changed meaning. In either case a new perspective results." (Gordon Allport, *Pattern and Growth in Personality* [New York: Holt, Rinehart & Winston, 1961]. Cf. also Allport's *The Individual and His Religion* [New York: Macmillan, 1950].)

comes from measuring each action and thought against what the individual ought to do to become the sort of person he wants himself to be.

A human being has the potential to mature in several ways. Physical maturity involves his attaining certain body size and muscular strength, developing systems for maximizing the struggle against entropic ruin (he must have some systemic resistance to both disease and degenerative deterioration), being capable of reproducing, and doing all this with sufficient inner harmony to be free of pain most of the time.

For a long time the sole definition of maturity concerned physical size and strength. The Homeric Greeks added cunning to this criterion, and the Periclean Greeks lived by the refined concept "a sound mind in a sound body." Thus mental maturity was recognized as separate from but interdependent with physical maturity.

Later civilizations learned that emotional maturity is important to the individual and his society, and that it is separate from both physical and mental states. Any community that has progressed beyond the point of ascribing aberrant behavior to demons or perversity can discern that a criminal may be of quite sound physical and mental state, but of arrested emotional development, which precluded the emergence of any kind of conscience. Gangster Al Capone opened soup kitchens in Chicago for hungry bums and on at least one occasion insisted on paying for the hospitalization of an innocent bystander injured in a burst of gang violence, but his desire to be liked and looked up to apparently was not based on any ability to empathize. When an employee of Colissimo's was accidentally killed during the assassination of Capone's uncle, Big Jim Colissimo, on Capone's order, Al ordered a small wreath of flowers for the widow from Dion O'Bannion's flower shop. When O'Bannion reminded him that the dead man left behind a large family, Capone is reported to have said cheerily, "Then make it a *big* wreath."

Diderot once observed that all children are essentially criminal. He might have added that when bodies and minds mature around childish emotional levels, the childish immaturities can gain great and disastrous scope.

Although physical maturity is a very complicated affair physiologically, it is not the concern of this book. For one thing, we understand it fully: Any intelligent person knows precisely what the term means. Moreover, its attainment is "automatic," given proper nutrition, access to modern medical techniques, and absence of congenital defects. Those unfortunates without adequate nutrition and medical care are victims of maldistribution, and that is a political and social problem.

Maturing *mentally* depends on a more complicated set of conditions, some of them, according to recent discoveries, obtaining during gestation and the first few days of birth; some of them environmental, involving early habits and patterns of learning; and still others intertwined with emotional factors. But still the layman's concern with acquiring purely *mental* maturity, in the sense of development of rational machinery sufficient to cope with the normal exigencies of life, is also of relatively limited importance to the thrust of this book. To clarify: By the same token that the largest, most powerful human may not necessarily be the most physically mature (he may have been damaged by a proneness to tuberculosis or cancer, or be unable to reproduce, or have fits or frequent incapacitating cramps and poor circulation, a musclebound condition, etc.), the "smartest" human may not necessarily be the most mentally mature. He may be brilliant but lack insight; he may be improperly motivated and employ his superb intellect in meaningless or self-defeating causes.

So the emphasis here is on *emotional* maturity as a proper concern, and it is fourfold: (1) it does involve motivation and self-actualization; (2) there are far fewer people who achieve this kind of maturity than the other kinds; (3) its potential is probably inherent in every human conceived and in every immature adult, obscured usually by conditions demonstrably changeable, and (4) in an age of rapid change and immense technological power, there is urgent need for both individuals and societies to seek this kind of maturity if human happiness and humanity itself are to continue on the earth.

This last point is true not only in democratic societies, and with respect to their foreign policies, but it applies as well to the direction taken by revolutions, the goals of business and technology, city planning, rescue from pollution and the depletion of natural resources, and the dangers of what philosopher John Wilkinson calls "a unitary social machine . . . being created, that has its own logic, ends, and imperatives, and that reduces to mere nostalgia all traditional human values."

Perhaps fortuitously, in the midst of peril, there are appearing evidences of corrective possibilities, or at least glimpses of possible new avenues of escape: techniques and tools of exploration such as psychiatry, chemotherapy (still new on the scene), chemical, psychedelic, and biofeedback, gateways to realms of the mind not yet dreamed of, let alone explored, and whole cultural movements of change. If the controls imposed on these currents of change are minimal—i.e., if they are designed to allow maximum freedom while preserving, not a status quo, but elements of tradition deserving to survive—they will be acceptable controls.

Where does society enter the circle, and how does it decide what elements of tradition should survive?

It requires maturity to tolerate rapid change; in turn, rapid change may be necessary to the new conditions for the blossoming of widespread maturity. The circle is vicious. On the one hand we thirst for stability—much as Plato, after a lifetime of freedom to bloody his head on the stone wall of logic, "envied the quiet orthodoxy of Egypt"—yet on the other hand we see that some drastic change is needed to head off a runaway technology. Whether or to what extent technology, particularly in its newly emergent cybernetic phase, with computers increasingly planning and making policy and setting goals, is necessarily a threat to human well-being, is a controversy that has gone on since before

Norbert Wiener coined the word "cybernetics," and my assumption that it is a threat is admittedly an opinion. Two excellent works on opposite sides of the argument are Jacques Ellul's *The Technological Society** and Charles Silberman's *The Myth of Automation*.† Although Silberman believes (and I yearn to agree with him) that safeguards such as education will protect the domain of free and rational human action, Ellul points out that *all* technical problems, including education, are increasingly met with technical solutions, and therefore abet the enslavement of man by the machine.

## [4]

By what mechanism does the maturing person adjust to changing environment while maintaining his integrity? C. W. Heath cites as a prime quality of maturity the possession of adaptive controls that permit continued growth while maintaining internal organization. A well-organized sailing vessel, to use an analogy, can set and trim sails according to conditions it can't control. In light airs it may set an enormous area of sail to take advantage of the slightest breath of wind. In flat calms it can lower boats and be pulled through a windless area by oarsmen. In storms it can keep way by reducing canvas to a small try-sail, and in the extremity of a hurricane it can run "under bare poles," dragging lines or a sea anchor so as not to broach or capsize, with a good chance of weathering the blow. It carries spare canvas and rope and building materials for the repair of damage, and although the boat may not "learn" from each experience, the chances are that its captain will.

A mature person can be theoretically described as a "stably organized individual who seeks out and is open to new experiences but who also has the capacity to resist and/or recover from the disorganizing influences of the disturbing information he encoun-

* New York: Knopf, 1964.
† New York: Harper & Row, 1966.

ters." Mature individuals are not immune to disorganizing influences. In fact, they are somewhat more likely to encounter them because of less fear on their part of experimenting, and of abandoning defense mechanisms.

How many mature humans are there in the world today? There is no scientific way of determining this. First of all, there is no agreement on, or ways of, measuring the degree or combination of traits required for even an arbitrary definition of the state, much less a means of taking a head count. Therefore the best that can be done is to make a rough count based on a guess, in turn based on an arbitrary definition of the term "mature," based in this case on the following tentative criteria (this is about as unscientific as we can get, but we've decided not to try to put ourselves into purely scientific methodology): (1) Patience: the ability to wait for or voluntarily defer rewards and to savor anticipation of rewards. (2) Empathy: the tendency to be emotionally moved by the plight of others more than one's own plight. (3) Realism: consciousness of mortality and acceptance of it, without morbid coloration by it. (4) Responsibility: understanding of the presence and role of volition in every conscious act.

*Patience.* A small child, promised a surprise or a reward a day or an hour from "now," spends some of the intervening time in torment over the delay. Unless his attention is drawn elsewhere, he will fret until the magic moment is at hand. He lacks the ability to tolerate waiting. After maturing somewhat he will be able to shelve his thought about the impending prize or event. At a higher level of maturity he will be able to think about the good thing and enjoy the anticipation. If he concentrates on this skill he may at one stage in life find that it can overreach the realization of the reward. If this becomes habitual it is evidence of an unrealistic attitude toward the goal; many plans and dreams are carried to inordinate heights, rendering the realities at the end of the dreams anticlimactic. But the healthy individual will be able to anticipate realistically with a pleasure proportionate to what he is anticipating. In the mature adult this pleasure can sometimes span years.

*Empathy.* Find out why a person cries, and something of his

maturity can be discerned. This has to do with an ability to empathize, but this is not the whole of the phenomenon. Along with
the development of feeling concerning others is the diminishing
of tears expended for oneself. In the shift from autocentrism
to allocentrism—that is, from self-centeredness to other-centered-
ness—the maturing person would seem to preserve a more or less
constant level of activity of the lachrymal glands. If a child mashes
his thumb with a hammer he is very likely to weep. Grown up, he
may only swear when this happens, even though there is considerable pain. At the same time he may cry at a funeral or a
theatrical offering. All tears may be idle, but maturity can be
measured by what makes them flow.

*Realism.* At some point in life the normal human wakes up to
the fact that there are so many hours in the day, so many days
and weeks in a year, and so many years in the average lifetime.
Unless he is deluded by abnormal defenses he has put up against
this fact, he admits to himself that one day in the future the sun
will rise and thereafter never rise again for him. Normal defenses
will spare him morbid brooding over the fact. A high degree of
maturity will render even these defenses unnecessary, and he will
live each day without dread or false hope of an indefinite stay.

Attitudes toward time are related in certain ways to maturing.
Most of us sense that time seems to run faster the older we get.
Generally this occurs only with respect to time *looked back on.*
William James refers to Professors Lazarus (*"Zeit und Weile,"*
*Ideale Fragen,* 1878) and Paul Janet (*Revue Philosophique,* Vol.
III) in writing:

"The same space of time seems shorter as we grow older—that
is, the days, the months, and the years do so; whether the hours do
so is doubtful, and the minutes and seconds to all appearances remain about the same."‡ The actual elapsing of a minute or a
month should be no different in old age than in youth. A greater
degree of maturity should free a person from any real feeling
that his event rate is accelerating. It is an illusion the roots of

‡ William James, *Great Books of the Western World,* "The Principles of
Psychology," Vol. 53 (Chicago: Encyclopaedia Britannica, 1952), p. 409.

which are probably in such factors as repetition of experiences and the mechanism of perceiving quantities in percentages. If you are seated in a room illuminated by a single candle and someone brings in another candle, you will notice an appreciable increase in the light. It won't seem to have doubled, but you will know it is brighter. If you are in the same room with ninety-nine lighted candles and someone brings in a hundredth candle, you probably would be unaware of the increase in light. And yet the hundredth candle adds as much light to the room as did the second. Perception involving proportion is not scalar. A two-year-old has lived half his life in the past year and is bound to count it longer than a single year to an octogenarian, whose rate of measurement judges the year to be one-eightieth of his life. Only in retrospect, when the quantity of a fragment of time is seen in the light of total experience, does the fragment seem to be less than its intrinsic value. This is an illusion, and a mature outlook sees it as an illusion and is not dismayed or tricked into thinking that time really speeds up on him.

Curiously, a high degree of maturity can recapture one valuable facet of subjective time enjoyed by the child and lost by the immature adult: that is the "eternal" flavor of each moment, as sensed by one who has not yet developed, or has freed himself from, a sense of dread. Tell a small child he has forty-five minutes to play before bedtime and that he must come in when you call him. He will enjoy forty-four minutes and fifty-nine seconds of play as though it were never coming to an end. True, he may be crushed when you call him in, but he will not have spoiled a moment of his play by thinking, "I've been out here about a half hour now—that means there's only a third of my playtime left. I'd better enjoy it." He will learn this later. And it may spoil a lot of vacations and visits for him. But if he matures enough to weed out dread, he will, without reinstating a childish vulnerability to endings, recapture the childlike quality of eternity in every savored moment.

*Responsibility.* No one ever does anything he doesn't want to do. I remember a discussion of this with a grown man some years ago during which, in denying the validity of the statement, he grew angry, twice broke off the conversation, and at the end was nearly in tears. It surprised me and set me to wondering why it was so important to him to believe the opposite: that people do things they don't want to do. I think it is important to many people, for a reason I will state presently. Phrases such as "I had no choice," or "I was forced to walk out of the meeting," or "You made me love you," all show a fallacy in human thinking so skill-fully camouflaged that it must be more than a misunderstanding of the meaning of volition; I suspect that it is more a persistent and nearly universal shield against knowing the real relation be-tween freedom and responsibility.

As an example, if a man reports to the highway police, "I was forced off the road," it could be true. If another vehicle, in con-tact with his, literally impelled him into the ditch, then he was truly forced off the road, and the incident was not the result of action on his part. But suppose he says (or meant by the state-ment, "I was forced off the road"), "I was forced *to drive* off the road." Now the statement is false. He may have been boxed into a very unpleasant set of alternatives, such as a choice between a head-on collision or getting off the road; or hitting a child or getting off the road; but if he made a decision and took action based on that decision, he was not forced. *No action is forced*. If action is taken, a set of choices is present (at least two alternative choices), and if no choice is present, the event does not involve action.

Further, it can be domonstrated that wherever there is aware-ness of available choice, action (that is, volition) is inevitable. Suppose a man points a gun at you and tells you to get out of the room or he will kill you. It is very easy to say later, "I had no choice" in explaining why you left the room. Again the statement is false. Faced with the situation, you have several choices: (1) you may try to talk the gunman out of carrying out his threat; (2) you may try to jump him and disarm him, hoping that you can do so before he can pull the trigger; (3) you may decide that neither of these choices is worth the chance involved and so walk out of the room, or (4) you can sit there and die.

Whatever action you take is the result of choosing and acting, with no escape from full responsibility for the action. So the statement, "I had no choice" is meaningless.

But now suppose a bouncer in a nightclub told you to leave, and when you refused he picked you up and threw you out. Here you *had* no choice, but neither did you initiate any action. To repeat: No one ever *does* anything he doesn't want to do. The alternatives available to him may be generally unattractive, and he may bitterly wish for things to be different. The alternatives may indeed be so bleak as to appear evenly matched, and the result of this evaluation may overwhelm his capacity to act. But abdication of volition is the act of putting the outcome in the hands of fate (flipping a coin, so to speak), and as such *is itself an act of volition*—one chooses, in effect, to initiate nonaction in this instance. This is a form of action since, as was said earlier, volition (and with it, responsibility) is inevitable wherever awareness of choice exists.

It should be pointed out that although an individual is totally responsible for each of his actions, he is not totally responsible for the outcome of these actions. This concept will help explain away the classic free will-and-determinism paradox. If action and responsibility are inseparable, and if awareness of choice and action are inseparable, then it follows that all three are rigidly linked and form a continuum in which the conscious individual is trapped.

If to be conscious is to be conscious of environmental choices, and to be conscious of choices is inevitably to act, and to act is to be automatically responsible for the action, then consciousness-action-responsibility becomes in a sense deterministic, and freedom of will is threatened.

To put it another way: If, faced with a set of choices, it is inevitable that you choose, and on choosing it is inevitable that you initiate *some* action, and automatically inevitable that you have full responsibility for such action, your freedom then seems less than complete. And if you are not completely free, can you be blamed for any state of affairs?

Is not freedom of action then a fiction? Arguments about determinism and free will are ancient.

The way out of this maze seems to me (and here I depart from the classic mode of arguing) to lie in the earlier statement that the individual, although totally responsible for each of his actions, is not totally responsible for the outcome of each action. If the bouncer throws you out of the nightclub, you may be acting all the while to prevent his throwing you out. But individuals are limited in strength, and he may be stronger than you. If so, your action may be in vain, and consequences can be forced on you for which you are not responsible. You are still fully responsible for your attempts to thwart eviction, but you may not succeed in them. In other words, you can fail in a given attempt. This fact of potential failure in any and every enterprise is the key to the preservation of free will. We are not omnipotent, and our very best efforts to assess a situation and implement an action can at times fail to produce a desired outcome.

For some curious reason the immature attitude tends to assume responsibility for the outcome where there are failures, and to dodge responsibility for actions. We seem always to feel guilty about the wrong things. We want to blame fate and the gods or other people for actions purely our own, but at the same time feel guilty about not being sufficiently strong to make the world over as we think it ought to be. In this we have the cart before the horse.

However, we are free to act.

If a man says, "I was forced to do this or that," thus denying responsibility by upholding determinism, one might ask him why he is at pains to prove he is not a free agent. Let him point out that he failed in accomplishment of his objective, or that he misappraised his situation, or even that he feels bad about the outcome, and we can sympathize with him and admire his honesty; but his actions were not and never will be forced. To repeat: We are free to act. And we do so even before we react. "The individual acts on its environment before it reacts to its environment."* The negative fact of potential failure in enterprise is the bulwark and substance of our freedom. In a later chapter, human limitations and their uses will be explored.

* Coghill, quoted by Charlotte Bühler, "Maturation and Motivation," *Dialectica* 5, 1951, pp. 312–61.

CHAPTER II

## How Many Potatoes Grow Large?

Attempting to answer the question, "How many people reach maturity?" is a little like asking, "How many potatoes grow large?" How large? I remember as a child my grandfather telling me of a prize-winning potato that just fit into a bushel basket and made a "bushel of potato." There have not been many such potatoes. There have not been many such humans as Gautama Buddha or Jesus of Nazareth. There have been somewhat more individuals at the level of Marcus Aurelius and Mahatma Gandhi and perhaps significant numbers like Pericles and Leonardo, though history does not necessarily memorialize the most mature of all men. It is at best a cloudy pastime trying to point to known names and arrange them into a pecking order of maturity. Many who made enormous contributions to humanity were obviously of uneven development. "Do we not all know immature people who are highly creative, heroic in special ways, and possessed of other desirable attributes? It seems that especially the value of *creativity* is present in many lives that are warped, retarded, even neurotic and psychotic. And the world needs creativity," says Gordon Allport in *Pattern and Growth in Personality*. There is a case to be made that creativity in artistic channels is given added drive through the needs brought on in the artist by his failure to mature. More-over, there is no clear and agreed formula, or means to test it, for determining the maturity of a living individual, let alone historic figures with sketchy or unreliable biographies. Freud, incidentally, published a psychoanalysis of Leonardo, applying his analytic tech-niques to biographical material and the legacy of Leonardo's art. Finally, although a highly mature person often has a magnetic quality that tends to attract disciples, the scope of attention thus gathered is deep rather than wide (unless an accident of fate makes his life the nucleus of a new cult), and countless numbers of mature humans may have come and gone beneath the surface of history without having sought or acquired acclaim. This quan-tity cannot be measured.

It requires no expertise to distinguish small potatoes from large ones. It is unlikely that many pumpkin-size potatoes have escaped notice. But many highly mature humans may have gone unre-corded. It is, however, safe to assume that fully mature humans have always been in something of a minority. Social development and behavior would surely be different from what we know it to have been throughout history if a majority of the population had reached maturity. If leadership were recruited from the wise in-stead of the power-hungry, nations and the world would have de-veloped along less bungling and bloody lines.

In speculating about percentages of people who mature, I can offer no promise of accuracy. But even if the guesses are off by whole orders of magnitude, the exercise serves a useful purpose. Let us use two sliding and virtually unknown variables that will be functions of each other. They are the questions, How mature? (degree), and How many at each level? (percentages and num-bers). Whether you go along with values selected here or substi-tute your own, some of the conclusions will be the same. Another nautical analogy is pertinent: a procedure in celestial navigation is the assumption of a position for the ship. It is purely arbitrary, and two different navigators, assuming the ship to be in different positions, miles apart, will eventually, if their sights and interpolations are accurate, arrive at the same corrected position, which is where the ship actually is.

Let us pick a level of maturity at which a human adult can absorb some education, can cope with family and job stresses without breaking down even though most of his emotional energy is spent in "just making it," and can succeed in getting through life without being hospitalized for psychopathological reasons. About 90 percent of the population of the United States reaches at least this level of maturity.

Next, consider the level at which a person has a fairly strong sense of initiative, feels he knows who he is, holds plans for self-improvement, expends most of his energies in work (at least some of it creative), is able to love more or less unconditionally (i.e., is fairly free of jealously and possessiveness), has a strong ethic by which he lives at least most of the time, feels "accepted" by other people, is not afraid to experiment, learns from encounters with disruptive influences, has what he feels is a good grasp of reality, has some genuine empathy (concerns himself with the rights and welfare of others), and is relatively independent of authority. At this level we might find 15 to 25 percent of U.S. citizens.

Still another and higher set of attributes: the person whose sense of "modesty" operates from a desire to avoid offending others rather than from any need of his own or sense of shame, whose freedom from conventionality shows in his willingness to break rules for reasons other than rebellion, who fears and hates no man, whose love is totally unconditional, whose morality stems from an inner ethic and who obeys man-made rules either where they coincide with his own or where expediency dictates and integrity is unharmed, who has no empathetic provincialism, and whose ego has atrophied to negligible or completely manageable size. This may be the one-in-a-thousand-to-one-in-ten-thousand person.

Let's try to picture now a human being who is the complete captain of his soul; who has "become his own mother and father"; who lives comfortably with authority but is in no way under any authority; who is completely self-actualizing; who has abandoned extrinsic religion, or transformed it to that "mature religious senti-

ment . . . accompanied by a generic conscience whose quality is
one of total directedness" (Allport); and whose "adjustment" to
his society in no way involves compromises with his personal
ethics. Here is a one-in-a-hundred-thousand-to-one-in-a-million
man. Socrates was one such, according to Plato; and Epictetus,
according to a disciple who wrote down the Enchiridion. Possibly
there have been only a few hundred such men, less celebrated
than these, but as mature.

Finally, if we are to extrapolate these traits to some kind of
limit, we can imagine a person who not only empathizes with
other living beings, but whose extension of self is tantamount to
participating in all life and the whole of the universe; whose ego is
completely dissolved; and whose consciousness is what Maslow
calls "oceanic" or what the West has (somewhat contemptuously)
termed "mystic." How many? A handful of ancients who forged
the Vedas and Upanishads, a few who started along with the
world's religions and rose above them. (Remember that Buddha
was not a Buddhist and Christ considered himself a Jew but broke
many Jewish rules in the interest of the higher ethic he sensed in
Judaism.)

Could there be a dozen alive today in a world of 3½ billion?

Assuming this imagined "limit" to be somewhere along the true
path of maturing, one of the obstacles to its attainment is that
it seems forbidding, for all the talk of the ecstasy that is supposed
to accompany its attainment. The caterpillar may not *wish* to get
into his cocoon although persuaded that he will emerge a butterfly,
because he has "never been a butterfly." Most of us will prefer to
cling to some vestiges of immaturity, for that is the nearly universal human condition. We fear the loneliness of heights.

# CHAPTER III

## Maturity and the Social Milieu

One might be justified in some optimism regarding progress in modern society if there were evidence that a higher percentage of humans come to reasonable maturity today than was the case in earlier times. But the modern world has a distressing tendency to conceive progress in terms of the increase of intelligence, and it does not necessarily follow that long-range human good will be served through increase of intelligence alone. In the same way that an emotionally stunted individual does not improve on merely getting "smarter" (in fact, he becomes more of a menace to his fellows), a society of relatively immature citizens will progress in possibly unwholesome ways with the mere development of its organization. Although some of today's thinkers believe that increased intelligence can point the way to whatever else is necessary to genuine progress for mankind, others take a dim view of the gradual evaporation of individual freedom and the congealing of that caprice of spirit that flourished in the Renaissance but that is barely traceable in today's world of committees and teams.

Joseph Tussman, Professor of Philosophy at the University of California's Berkeley campus, thinks that higher development of human intelligence will be sensitive to problems and dangers and "could be brought to bear on purging the art of organization of its primitive inadequacies," as he put it in a discussion with members of the Center for the Study of Democratic Institutions at Santa Barbara, California.

Reason, in the opinion of philosopher Scott Buchanan, is "essentially intelligence, sensitive intelligence and not [a] crude, cruel thing. . . ."

John Platt of the University of Michigan sees hope in "limiting factors" probably inherent in processes in society that can be thought of as "multiple interconnected chain reactions." He says, "I believe that the mere re-statement of the reform problem in terms of self-amplification puts it in a new light. For by amplification, I mean what can be called technically 'a social chain reaction with positive feedback.' . . . Biochemists have long taken this view in describing processes in a biological organism. Occasionally one sees the notion of a chain reaction applied to such social processes as the growth of science or technology, but sociologists and political scientists seem not to have emphasized the concept very much so far. Certainly they seem not to have worked out the full implications of the analogy, with its rich and suggestive auxilliary concepts, such as 'critical size,' 'multiplication factors,' 'stability and instability'—depending on 'negative or positive feedback'—'exponential decay' and 'exponential growth' and the important concept of manipulation and control by 'control rods.' Monetary theory does make use of a number of these concepts, including the concept of control, and a few of the concepts are also used casually sometimes in describing the exponential growth of belligerence between powerful states up to the point of a runaway explosion. I believe the chain reaction analogy, including the control problem, needs to be explored much more thoroughly in these cases. I also believe that it can be applied profitably to less spectacular social phenomena such as the growth and decline of whole cultures, or the formation of schools of art, or to social reform and social change in general."*

Historian Arnold Toynbee, not too sanguine about human

* John R. Platt, *The Step to Man* (New York: Wiley, 1966), p. 41.

ability to save humanity from accelerating and dimly understood forces, thinks the universe still has some tricks up its sleeve, and looks to some higher power to initiate and sustain a countervailing trend. But this is a form of optimism. Not all the thinkers are this optimistic.

As a dispenser of gloom, George Orwell, in his *1984*, is downright vapid when compared with the authentic ring of doom in Rod Seidenberg's voice:

> The phenomenon of organization is rapidly permeating the entire panorama of modern civilization like a universal dye. . . . Organization breeds organization; thus, it constitutes a principle moving inexorably toward universality. In the function of any system, social or mechanical, efficiency demands that all anarchic elements be converted into component parts of a harmonious whole. Accordingly, the diverse phases of civilization are under constant pressure to enter into and harmonize with the dominant trend of events. In our highly structured civilization organization is the basic means for the functioning of all other means, and its expansion into every aspect of our social existence is implicit in the conduct of our affairs under the guiding principle of intelligence. This is merely to say that organization is implicit in the conscious adjustment of specific means toward the attainment of specific ends. It is significant in the context of our mechanized world that these terms apply precisely to the design of the machine. Indeed the machine exemplifies in its most pristine form the nature of organization: the effective arrangement of means in the pursuit of specific ends. This identity of logical structure represents more than a coincidence. It explains, in fact, the relatively sudden and universal appearance of organization as a necessary principle of operation in the modern world. . . . The autonomy of the individual, however, is doomed to shrink as society becomes ever more highly organized. At length the individual as such will have vanished in the anonymity of the mass. Perfect organization implies universal organization, since its functioning, like that of the machine, is contingent upon complete predictability. Hence it must in

principle extrude all idiosyncrasy, all spontaneity, all varia-
tion from established and explicit norms. Human beings must
become as predictable in every aspect of their lives as the machines they operate. Otherwise they are like grains of sand in
the mechanism—obstructing, defying, confusing the clarity
of its operation. Nor is this all. Under pressure of the drift
toward conformity, the very soil of individualism—particularly in its higher manifestations—is systematically leached of
its nutriment until the individual can no longer sustain himself and must lose all identity. Thus shrivelled, he remains an
isolated and meaningless discard from another age, if indeed
he is granted survival in a system of things ever more hostile
to his being.†

Even anthropologist-philosopher Teilhard de Chardin, whose
view of the future is bright with a glow of potential, is at pains
to point out that vigilance and effort are called for to fulfill any
kind of positive human destiny. At any turn, the drying up of such
caution and effort could let the whole thing go down the drain.
There is no cosmic guarantee that all will be well, no divine
imperative that outer darkness may not yet inherit all our efforts
and strivings on a moment's notice. The reins of evolution, according to Teilhard, have been taken over by man.

If this is so, it would seem that our chances of assuming the
responsibility would certainly be enhanced by setting up conditions under which great numbers of humans might fully mature.
It may be of no cosmic importance whether we continue to evolve,
or continue as a species, but if it is deemed important by so much
as one single individual, he need seek no further justification for
his personal assumption of social responsibility. It is in this inwardness that all meaning, personal and social, appears to some
to have its roots. Although it is not what could be called a trend
(in the sense of operating in the mainstream of Western life),
there are increasing numbers in Western civilization, particularly
among the young, who have recoiled from the hypocrisies and

† Roderick Seidenberg, "The Future: Some Basic Doubts," Conference on
Freedom and Justice in a Technological Society, May, 1966, Center for the
Study of Democratic Institutions, Santa Barbara, California.

injustices of their society, and in seeking some answer, have turned inward. The drug culture cannot be explained away as mere self-destructiveness. Some of it can be seen as the Western will to experiment, applied to Eastern realms previously explored by the more difficult and disciplined methods of asceticism, meditation, etc.

Is "inner space," as it has been called, a realm of greater meaning? Is "inwardness," generally, an important thing to consider? Consider a poet who, while flying alone in a small airplane, thinks of a poem. But before he can write it down for anyone else to enjoy, his plane crashes and he is killed, his new poem dying with him. Does it matter whether or not he had thought of the poem? Did the poem have any existence whatever? Now suppose we put the poet on a large airliner and give him a chance this time to write out his poem and to read it to a few other people, who enjoy it. But the trip ends disastrously with all aboard killed. The only surviving information is the sealed tape taken from the wreckage and bearing the last words of the pilot, who did not record the poem. Does it matter whether or not the poet wrote the poem or whether or not a handful of people, now dead, enjoyed it?

Once again (and let's deal a better hand to our poet this time), he thinks of his poem, along with many poems, writes them down, publishes them, lives to a ripe old age enjoying critical and popular acclaim, becoming poet laureate of his country, and finally is conceded to be the best poet the world has ever produced. Millions enjoy his poems, and his fame is a trail many times as long as his life span. But in time mankind changes, or vanishes without having perfected space travel, and in a few billion years the planet (which is after all a spaceship with long-term but finite life-support systems and supplies, and a few billion passengers) perishes in the paroxysm of an expanding sun, all poems, paintings, thoughts, and achievements going with it. Does it matter that he thought of the poem, or that few or many enjoyed it? The answer, according to those whose religious feelings are oriented to immanence rather than transcendence, is that nothing matters for any external reason whatever. But for internal reasons everything matters intensely—infinitely. The simplest thought or feeling is of ultimate importance, whether shared or not.

Therefore, if we create a work of art or perform a good deed in order to gain status or to bolster an ego image, or for any external reason at all, it is an empty and vain act. But the thought in itself, however private, like the *ding an sich*, the thing in itself, has meaning. The poem was meaningful, even if no one else ever heard or read it.

Whether or not we subscribe to this particular outlook, we can agree that personal maturity would appear to be desirable to almost everyone. Luella Cole, in her book *Attaining Maturity*,‡ entitles her second chapter "The Advantages and Disadvantages of Maturity." She lists among disadvantages "loneliness" and the necessity of "facing consequences." From the perspective of maturing, these become "alone-ness" and "responsibility," and are not so forbidding as they appear from below. I remember as a child not wanting to grow up. On a summer evening I would invite my father to join me in a footrace to the corner and back, but he would decline in order to settle himself into the porch swing to read the paper. I could not then imagine the satisfaction of rest after a hard day's work, or that the contents of a newspaper could have any interest for anyone.

Surely there is a greater opportunity for the individual to mature emotionally now than in those earlier human societies where constant danger, heavy taboos, a hostile pantheon, and rule by fear weighed down each human from the moment of his birth. And yet we were not, as a species, consigned to universal and perpetual insanity, which could easily have been our lot according to some current psychological theories. Nor are we as prone to mature now in an age of relative enlightenment and freedom from want, fear, and oppression, as standard psychological ideas would indicate we should.

One reason for this latter state may be that we are brought up in an atmosphere of immaturity. We think of mental health as

‡ New York: Farrar and Rinehart, 1944.

the mere absence of mental illness. Anyone who does not need a psychiatrist or psychologist has no reason to strive for emotional improvement. So he strives for money, or fame or power, or he struggles with boredom while acquiring more leisure. He leaves social good and human progress to the "do-gooders" and sees no need and often no room to improve his own inner condition. MIT's Huston Smith has said, "There is one point that Indians have seen far more clearly than we have: that the subconscious, besides being pathological, can also be healthy. When it is, it works for us beyond the powers of the conscious mind, balancing to a degree the damage it can do if it is pathologic. The West has tended to forget that doctors deal with sick people; as a doctor, Freud dealt mainly with sick subconscious minds and he gave us a brilliant typology of the ways in which the pathological subconscious can create trouble. But what is equally true, that the 'subconscious' can work in our behalf when it is healthy, perhaps only the frontier scientist and the really creative artist in the West understand."

In Elizabethan England few people kept their teeth beyond the age of forty. The nutrition was so abysmal that vitamin deficiency and scurvy robbed them of the dental equipment with which to handle what food they had. They accepted this as a more or less standard human condition. But not all people lost their teeth. Occasional titans of physical health appeared, who, by accidents of birth and chemical makeup, coupled with access to nutritive elements suitable to them, enjoyed robust health well into advanced years. These people were rare.

In a somewhat parallel way, our societies today, all of them, are short on the nutrients essential to full emotional maturation. In spite of this, some few individuals, lucky enough to embody a certain type of inner makeup and to enjoy the right type of early environment, and above all to have developed both a deep sense of security and a habit of efficiently deploying adaptive resources for environmental excursions, learning from each encounter, manage to reach some rarefied plateaus of maturity.

I think they have increased now in numbers, at least on the

level of what we may call reasonable maturity; but only slightly more. I further believe that these increases, whatever they are, have little effect on the course of human progress as yet, but that as they approach a critical percentage, a near-saturation point, they will impart to humanity a whole new complexion. It is at this point that we may expect to see sudden, perhaps even explosive, social progress, analogous to the explosive character of technical progress touched off by the advent of the machine.

Whether in the meantime, with a widening gap between the two, mature individuals can do much to help to hold everything together remains to be seen. Our proposition is that the mature individual can get more out of life and put more into it than an immature one, whether his social environment is threatening and threatened or serene and secure.

# CHAPTER IV

## *Communicating*

### [1]

In the same way that genius and madness are popularly imagined
to be closely identified, innocence and enlightenment have some
apparent similarities in spite of their being at opposite ends of a
spectrum of possible human development. The steps along the way
must be traversed by every person who matures, but we shall see
that in several aspects of maturing, an individual appears to recapture some of the qualities of early childhood.

A human embryo is in a sense enlightened, in that his ability to
cope matches his environment, and his desires match to a certain
extent his condition. As far as we know, he is not puzzled or frustrated, he is secure, he is constantly growing, not stagnating, and
there is no threat to the supply of his needs. In this he may re-
semble the sage, who does not trouble himself with particulars,
whose desires are under such control he can't be thwarted by external circumstance, who is open to growth without fear. The
parallel is striking even though one condition requires ignorance,
and the other, wisdom.

At birth the infant is faced with gigantic problems, and he sets
about immediately to cope with them. Instinct serves him in the
most immediate ones. His oxygen supply is cut off with the sever-

ing of the umbilical cord, and he will from this moment to the
end of his life be only minutes away from death unless he pumps
air in and out of lungs that are at the moment of birth clogged
with mucus. He does not have to learn or be taught how to
breathe. The nutritive fuel he will burn in his body with this air
must be taken in through his mouth, and he will have to swallow
it. He does not have to be taught how to swallow. But very nearly
everything else he must do—every technique he will have to acquire in order to function—will be mastered by learning, and only
with some conscious effort on his part. He is, at the moment, a
fantastic potential, a great lump of promise. He has a more or less
decent chance of growing up, depending on where and to whom
he is born, a better-than-even chance of living some years as an
adult with a preponderance of pleasure and relatively little pain,
and a slim chance of really maturing along all significant lines.

There are many steps he must take to ripen.

[2]

The newborn human sets out on the strangely circular path of
developing extensions of his "self."

At the beginning he is completely self-centered, even though he
has no clear idea what pieces of the world are part of him and
what are not. In learning this he develops an ego, which he may
one day dismantle, if he goes far enough in maturing. (Here again
the vague similarity between the infant and the sage. To cope
with the world it is necessary at first to distinguish between the
"me" and the "not me" however fictional such a distinction may
later be shown to be.) Having separated himself from the rest of
the world at the boundary of his skin, the infant now sets about to
establish relationships with other things along certain conventional
channels—things possessing power for good and harm. Some of
the things are animated and similar to him but larger and clev-
erer than he. Mother is one of those things. She can hold, protect,
feed, soothe, and guide. By steps a sense of approval-disapproval

emerges; also the sense of a world populated by several other beings identifiable by sight and authority (and finally by personality), bearing the labels "daddy" and "sister" and "brother" and
"doggy."

At first crying is a reflex, but the infant soon learns it brings
Mother, and her presence is linked in a short time to the mysterious correction of whatever discomfort caused the crying. It may
seem accidental the first few times, but very quickly he learns of
the cause-effect relationship of this set of events and can trigger
it with his own will. This establishes an early volitional link with
the outside world. From here on, as he learns other ways to act,
and as he learns that some acts produce rewards and others punishment, he is on the way to the development of a technique for coping. Later on, patterns become apparent to him that shape the
foundations for a social consciousness on which he can build both
a formula for expedient and efficient behavior and an empathetic
sense that will enable him to develop affection, sympathy, and a
sense of willing sharing. But the path is circular, because he com-
mences in the direction of separating himself from the rest of the
world, making his concept of himself an isolated particular in a
world viewed as isolated particulars, and then after a time, beginning to establish links with other things and people that will
eventually become real extensions of self and that will unify the
particulars, himself included, into groups and classes and wholes.
Unless this unifying process is arrested at a socially primitive
level, he will escape or outgrow what Harry Overstreet calls "empathetic provincialism," a condition brought on by the tendency
to isolate first self, then family and clan, tribe and city, state and
nation.

This propensity for drawing boundaries and viewing everything outside with hostility is unfortunately reinforced in many
social situations and institutions. Schools, churches, and patri-
otic organizations coin phrases such as "the true faith" or "one of
us," etc., making an implied blanket indictment of those not inside the perimeter of the class considered "it." Sometimes the
pejorative light thrown on outsiders is more than merely implied.

Nearly every ethnic group has or at one time had a specific term for men not of their kind ("Jew and Gentile," "Greek and barbarian," "Christian and infidel," "American and foreigner"). Go to the remotest Indian or Eskimo tribe and you will likely find a set of terms meaning essentially "we the people" and "them bums." In *The Mature Mind* Overstreet says, "Many people who would suffer the humiliation of a friend or even of a stranger who belonged to their own class or race, as though it were their own, will remain indifferent to the humiliation of a member of a different class or race. They are quite literally unable to believe that this 'outsider' actually has the same feelings that they and their kind experience. It is this type of provincial imagination that accounts for the perennial capacity of many people to be the kind within the family circle and yet indifferent to sufferings of people outside that circle; to be strictly honest in dealing with members of their own class and yet shrewd and ruthless to the point of dishonesty when they extend their influence across class lines."*

[3]

Small wonder that the young person finds a block to maturing fully in the contradictory values of his cultural environment. He is encouraged to be "for" other people if they are members of his group and "against" them if they are outsiders or competitors; he is told "Thou shalt not kill," but is explained that this does not apply to condemned criminals or the enemy in war. He is expected to develop empathy as an extension of himself for reasons desirable to society, but at the same time he is discouraged from applying it in any universal sense.

He is, in short, expected to rise to the level of maturity represented by his community or its rules, but no higher. If momentum or vital drive propels him farther up he may threaten cherished prejudices, and become a candidate for pruning. The confusion of these limitations, if not overcome by a further maturing than most

* H. A. Overstreet, *The Mature Mind* (New York: Norton, 1949).

societies will permit, will produce hostility harmful to himself if the individual becomes neurotic, and to society if he should become psychotic. He may of course escape severe warp and become a force for pulling up the standards of his community if he is socially or politically oriented, or fits into what Spranger calls social or political value-types; or he may withdraw from activist efforts in favor of a contemplative life, retaining his ideas of what ought to be, if he tends more toward a theoretical or aesthetic outlook.

Carl Binger, approaching the subject from an operational point of view, examines what the mature individual is capable of doing: "First, is he able to plan for the future? Can he wait for his satisfaction to come in due course or does he insist on immediate gratification? In other words, can he tolerate a reasonable degree of frustration and is he flexible enough and adaptable enough to change his attitude in order to conform with the exigencies of life? (A mature person should be able to do all these things without loss of self-control and without excessive display of emotion.) And furthermore, can he behave in this adult fashion even if he has himself in hand, without too much strain and without developing too much anxiety?"

The last question spotlights one of modern society's most sinister problems. Where increasing strain in the individual is apparent by the overflow of neurotic outbursts, the course of his disorder can be traced with some degree of accuracy by his associates, who are put on their guard against any really hostile action. This aberrant behavior may or may not in itself relieve or mitigate the strain (it may at least seem to do so indirectly by his being persuaded to seek therapy). But not all strain is so easily detected by nonprofessionals. We know that too often a festering emotional illness builds up beneath a membrane of normal behavior that not only conceals the condition but prevents any escape of pressure. Then when the blowup comes, it is ferociously destructive to a social environment totally unaware of the approaching danger.

Case histories are full of "quiet" youths, "model students," polite, soft-spoken adults, fully rational and often compliant in social and personal behavior, who suddenly went amok and killed people. Profiles of assassins and skyjackers often fit these types.

These human *supernovae*, disintegrating in the explosion of pent-up hate and rage, are rare enough to give us some statistical safety against death from such accidents, but there is an apparent increase in violence in many of the world's societies, and it is not, in my opinion, attributable solely to more thorough reporting. Increasing emotional disorders are alarming enough to any community, but if there is a significant rise in the kind of destructive illness that remains camouflaged until it explodes, a problem exists of far greater magnitude. It is appropriate to ask if there is something about the society itself and its customs that induce individuals under strain to become walking emotional bombs.

[4]

The newborn human embarks instantly on a course of learning. Without a constantly growing storehouse of knowledge, he will not mature. Although the compilation of facts and development of skills will not in themselves bring about the kind of maturity we are talking about, they are necessary steps to achieving the functions and techniques of growth.

The interdependence of mental and emotional processes is seen in the fact that severe or even mild brain damage can prevent the development of the rational machinery necessary to the acquiring and arranging of knowledge essential to the building of emotional maturity. Likewise, severe emotional warp early in life can inhibit the use of otherwise sound mental (rational) machinery. If this machinery is blocked enough in its efforts to gather knowledge, it will atrophy. Even if it goes on functioning well, emotional scars may prevent the individual's using the stored knowledge with any insight.

The newborn human articulates his needs at first by accident— by reflex and instinct (mother appears when he cries); later by will and habit (he can command her presence by crying); still later by language. The reception accorded his earliest efforts to communicate is an enormous factor in the patterns he will set up for building his vocabulary and the speed with which he will acquire his communicating technique. Maybe no other area of life is as frustrating to the individual as these earliest efforts to express himself. For one thing, his thoughts certainly outrun his available words. For another, his early thoughts are not structured. Raw feelings, nameless moods, desires, joys, discomforts, even insights well up from inside and overlap. Differentiation among these is of a continuous nature rather than discrete. Only later will the matrix of an acquired language force artificial shapes and boundaries on these early thoughts. To a certain extent, the very tool of articulation, language, will tend to circumscribe the truth of ideas by warping them into words. In one of William Saroyan's novels a small child found an egg and brought it to his mother. Holding it up to her, he sought to express what he knew about the egg. She waited patiently but never heard his truth. He couldn't express it, and "by the time he was old enough to give it expression, he would have forgotten it." But until we come up with something better than language for the expression of thoughts and the transmission of information, we will have to continue to cram our ideas and feelings into these little semantic pigeonholes, hoping some meaning will be carried along in the process.

But no matter how indirectly language conveys meaning—no matter what its limitations—speech is our common means of participating in a community of experience: a bridge to others that keeps us from being isolated. It is also, in its recorded form, our means of accumulating knowledge and consolidating gains.

[5]

One of the areas in which humans have felt most isolated, very often through whole lifetimes, is in the expression of sex urges. Why have so many diverse social attitudes impeded understanding in this area? Ignorance and prudery are not limited to Puritan and Victorian societies.

Perhaps it is because, along with expressing love, transmitting life, and yielding flashes of intense personal pleasure, sex is such a powerful troublemaker. The ancient Scythians were said to have copulated in public, but few durable societies have been this relaxed (and I suspect that even the Scythians' behavior was more ritualistic than naturalistic). Even primitive communal societies, uncluttered with concepts of inheritance, legitimacy, chastity, etc., still had and have a great deal of trouble handling sex easily as a personal and social problem. No human society on the earth today fails to embody in its tribal knowledge a connection between sexual intercourse and reproduction. Wherein this is seen as a connection between universal, powerful urges and mysterious results, the idea of magic comes into play. Since there is even at very early levels of community organization, a priest class to dominate and control the public, and since magic is the most potent tool to wield to this end, it is natural that sex is early involved with heavy taboos and rituals.

But there may be more mundane reasons for the darkness that persists on this subject, even in otherwise enlightened societies. The strangest and strongest taboos on sex are characterized by an *atmosphere of silence*. Very few things touching human existence are so awesome that they cannot be discussed—that they are driven into the collective subconscious. But it amounts very nearly to that in the case of sex. Objective field research has been so difficult that modern science accomplished nothing in studying the facts until quite recently. Not until after the midpoint of the twentieth century was anything published for the general public that represented a really scientific investigation of the physiology of human sex activity (notably *Human Sexual Response* by Masters and Johnson).

Physical privacy is important to the individual for complex reasons. The body processes are, for one thing, our sharpest reminder that we are animals, and that we are vulnerable and mortal. Observation or even discussion of someone else's body processes produce in us feelings ranging from boredom to revulsion, so we reason rightly that others may feel the same toward ours, and we contrive to behave in such a way as to spare them a tiresome ordeal, and ourselves the embarrassment and hurt of a kind of rejection. Even so, body processes, from breathing to digesting food and eliminating waste, are not kept quite as private from community attention as sexual activity. And the rules connected with sex produce some strange codes. For example, a married man will sometimes avoid mention of relations with his wife to a point of implying denial when a specific incident is involved, for example, in the not-unusual situation of two couples on a camping trip, with one couple "taking a walk" and the other "taking a nap." Yet the same man would be horrified if anyone thought his children were not really his, so he wants us to know he sleeps with his wife. It is this complicated and ambiguous nature of so many codes of sex behavior that set them apart from codes relating to other body functions.

This may be, in part at least, because sex is both personal and interpersonal. There is someone else to consider. Outside of auto-sexual activity, all sex is plural. There is gallantry as well as shyness in shielding a mate from the public leer.

Moreover, the consequences of sex are so much more far-reaching than those of any other physical function. This is the source of supply of humanity. A nightclub entertainer used to close his act with the line, ". . . and please be careful in your car; remember, most people are caused by accidents." Accidental pregnancy, even in permissive or understanding social environments, is a source of considerable long-range difficulty. In rigid, restrictive societies it brings permanent disgrace and ruin. The very subject has, at points in history, been so dangerous as to be painful—and painful things are suppressed.

On an individual level, privacy in sexual activity may be rooted deep in our animal past. Because of the physiological nature of the sex act, as well as the anatomical involvement, man as an animal is particularly vulnerable at that moment in case of attack from an enemy. It is conceivable that the instinct for privacy is therefore partly an instinct for self-preservation.

Finally, people have difficulty fitting their own individual feelings into a community of feelings. This may be more true of sexual feelings than any others because of their special depth and power. Young people often think their feelings are unique, and the secrecy of the community in matters of sex reinforces this idea. In no other area does the individual tend so to feel unique.

Sympathizing with someone else's sexual problems is difficult. (I would imagine that a "dirty old man" would never see himself as such—his thoughts are natural and necessary and perhaps, to him, beautiful.) The power of sex frightens us into isolation, and the isolation in turn seems to give it inordinate power.

It is hard to place the cart and the horse properly in this instance. Freud discovered that sex drives are not only powerful, widely permeating other areas of emotional life, but that they are manifested very early. Despite subsequent critical reappraisals of Freud's theories of sex (some of them taking him to task for using the word sex), the fact remains that he identified a powerful element in human growth—one that can be considered not only vulnerable to emotional warps, but a prime cause of them.

Part of the darkness still shrouding the whole subject lies in the fact that sexual immaturity is so prevalent that it is taken for normal. Although we are now sophisticated enough to see the homosexual, the sadist, the child molester, and the superprude as being emotionally disordered, we haven't yet arrived at a socially wholesome attitude toward the sex athlete, the edgy, overproud male, the Don Juan, the overdependent, the jealous and possessive, the ruthless, etc. Popular myths about menopause and prostate trouble and potency and masturbation still abound, and as long as we worship pinup love goddesses, as long as James Bond and other empathetic aesthetes are our screen heroes, as long as our repressions continue to show up in obsession with violence, both vicarious and (of late) real, we are not living in an environment of sexual maturity, and the favorable conditions for the maturation of individuals are diminished.

To mature sexually, psychologists tell us, the infant must move through stages of diffuse potential, early attachments (usually to grownups of the opposite sex), pre-adolescent homosexuality, intense adolescent heterosexuality involving generally short-term liaisons or fantasies with others of the same age, and finally to a plateau of stable relationship "with a loved partner" in which physical and emotional drives are channeled without undue difficulty.

Badly handled emotional experiences of the very young—jealousies and attachments—can become sources of guilt, hostility, and self-doubt. Although lives have been ruined by such experiences, they need not always be fatal to sound development.

# CHAPTER V

## Emotional Self-Healing

[1]

What evidence is there that emotional wounds, at least of certain types and degrees, tend to heal themselves? And are there things we can do to help such a natural process?

Our emotional machinery has more automatic recuperative power than is generally imagined (it is analogous to an untended cut healing itself). There are things we can do on our own to correct some types of emotional injuries (analogous to cleansing and bandaging one's own wound); and even when both the automatic healing process is overwhelmed and the volitional apparatus (self-help) is inadequate to correct disorders, professional help can do real wonders in many cases. This is analogous, though only roughly, to getting a doctor to set a broken bone or reset a crookedly healed one.

We are still too far from having sufficient knowledge of our deepest nature to eradicate all old scars in grownups or to prevent all emotional injuries to new humans, but it seems to me that much could be done that isn't being done—much that lies within our power.

Mark Twain once told of a man who languished for years in a dismal dungeon scheming how to get out by tunneling underground, prying bars out of a high window, or cutting through the wall. Suddenly he rose, opened the door, and walked out to freedom. It may be that the plight of many of us is similar. We conclude there is nothing we can do to correct some condition that is imprisoning us, or we read self-help books, expecting that they will hand us an instant solution, or we go to doctors and say, "Cure me." These procedures do not work. When they appear to do so, it is invariably because another element was also present.

To call this other element motivation is inaccurate. We are motivated by outside forces, and thus motivation is really *reaction*. "Self-motivation" might come nearer to the target, but this includes caprice or raw imagination, which may be creative, but is not always problem-solving; and I want to demonstrate a relationship between the desire to correct an inner condition and the initiation of an action or chain of actions that tends to accomplish the correction.

The term I've coined for this is "oblique volition." It requires diverting attention from the center of the problem and, almost haphazardly, trying peripheral gambits, many of which may be logical impossibilities. This is not unlike locating faint stars at night by not looking straight at them. The center of vision in the human eye is a little less sensitive to light than the regions immediately adjacent. If you look directly at a faint star it may disappear. You can relocate it by looking away to the side just slightly.

Sometimes when we try to work on our own mind *with* our own mind (a bit like lifting ourselves by our bootstraps), we conclude quite reasonably that it can't be done. If then, instead of either giving up or attempting to will some state by sheer volition, we try impossible but vaguely related ploys—that is, if we stab mentally around the periphery of the problems—we sometimes hit paydirt. The answers thus stumbled onto are usually connected with changes in attitude, but in emotional problems attitudinal change is what is most often desired. If it requires physical or rational changes and will not be satisfied without them, it is a physical or mental problem.

Let us say you are out in the rain getting wet and you don't want to get wetter. To make it stop raining is a physical problem, and it is properly viewed as impossible. To avoid getting wet is not necessarily a matter of making it stop raining. Although no desire or volition on your part will propitiate gods or manipulate clouds so as to control the rain, you can open your umbrella and solve the problem obliquely.

Some emotional problems are similar to this. The question posed can be a real stone wall against which all your best efforts are fruitless. Then at the moment you conclude there is no satisfactory answer, you resolve the problem by *changing the question*. For example, I knew of a man, the victim of extremely bad luck in the loss of his wife and three children in an auto accident, who in the agony of his grief framed the very human and understandable question, "To whom can I turn for comfort?" Indeed, could anyone on this earth make good his loss, or do anything at all to make him stop grieving? No answer seemed adequate to solve his problem, or to help save his sanity. But he found an answer in an unexpected place. He said that it came to him in the change of a single word. He heard the question, once, in his mind, as, "To whom can I turn *with* comfort?" This started a train of thought that developed into the knowledge that his grief was convertible into efforts on behalf of people whose problems were susceptible of understanding and love, and he became a volunteer worker at a mental hospital. As he grew to care about the individuals he was helping, he re-established his interest in life, came to feel he was in a sense dedicating his efforts to the memory of those he'd lost, and overcame his grief.

It was a solution, and it came from "oblique volition" rather than by a frontal attack, which would have been unavailing. Whether it was "God" or chance or autosuggestion that caused the substitution of the preposition "with" for "for" in his original question is not pertinent. What is pertinent is that he seized on it and built out of it a solution for himself. Oblique volition may sometimes be no more than editorial selection from a random

flow of elements—the seizing on the new concept being an act
of will. The problem is that many of us do not move to grab
possible solutions obliquely, because they are disguised and we
do not recognize them as desirable, or related, or even possible,
solutions. Self-motivation and self-actualization are not matters of
careful intellectual weighing of factors so much as the *act of
seizing on* factors.

A young man, named in the will of a rich uncle, found that he
had inherited a job in one of his uncle's banks, plus the contents
of a safe deposit box in one of the bank's vaults. Two keys were
required to open the box—one kept at the bank, the other in the
possession of the subscriber. As a banker he held one key already.
But his uncle's will had indicated that the other key was in the
box. The bank contended that this was impossible, since it took
both keys to lock as well as unlock the safe deposit box. His
anguish was intensified by knowledge that as a bank employee he
had automatic access to half of the necessary keys, although as
a subscriber he could not use the bank's key without producing
his own. The young man was certain his uncle had left him
something more than the bank job. Faced with this dilemma and
almost despairing of ever getting his inheritance, he started searching for the other key, reasoning that his uncle had set a test for
him, deeming him worthy only if he solved the problem. He
reread the will, questioned relatives, and studied his uncle's life
and papers to find a clue. But there was no real clue. There were
many false clues and false hopes through the years, and as time
wore on he despaired. Among the opinions of others on the
matter, the most distressing was that probably the other key was
indeed irretrievably inside the vault. How cruel it made his uncle
seem, to make it impossible for him ever to get his inheritance!
More years passed.

Let's imagine that the young man (now no longer young) decided at last to try the impossible: to get into the bank safe
deposit box without both keys. Imagine his surprise when he
discovered it required only the one key that he had all along. His

uncle had left his half unlocked. Inside was the other key, as un-necessary as half of our rules and beliefs.

The world imprisons us with conventional ideas.

## [2]

Try the impossible. Think the unthinkable. Entertain any idea that comes to you. If it is impossible, you will have confirmed your appraisal of it. Even if you entertain it and elect not to act on it, your decision will be on a sound basis; you will have actively *chosen* not to do it.

Think about doing something completely repugnant to you, horribly "unthinkable." I submit that if you reject such an idea after *seriously* considering it, you will be less likely to do it under some emotional stimulus than if you never let yourself explore the merits of the idea. True freedom of thought as well as true morality require that there be freedom of choice and no "unthinkable thoughts."

For example, consider seriously these things (even though none may attract you):

1. Joining the Communist Party.
2. Murdering a rich relative (particularly one whose will you are fairly sure includes a generous gesture toward you).
3. Sleeping with your neighbor's wife (or husband).
4. Blowing your job and your life savings for a month in Aruba.
5. Committing suicide.
6. Joining a lynch mob (i.e., killing for kicks).
7. Scolding a policeman or judge if his behavior warrants.
8. Taking drugs.
9. Getting roaring drunk.
10. Salting your next public remarks with four-letter words.
11. Becoming an atheist.

12. Listening carefully to your child's views on music and politics.
13. Selling everything you own and giving the proceeds to the poor.
14. Stealing a car.
15. Marrying outside your race.
16. Urging your daughter (or sister) to marry outside her race.
17. Having intercourse with your parent.
18. Joining the American Nazi Party.
19. Engaging in a homosexual act, or an infrahuman relationship.
20. Eating human flesh.
21. Changing occupations within the next thirty days.
22. Getting through an ice-cold shower.
23. Skipping two consecutive meals.
24. Dropping any grudge you're holding, regardless of how right you are.
25. Moving to an island in the South Pacific.
26. Joining a nudist colony.

You have probably done a few of these things, and considered several. This list of activities is set down for you to gauge yourself through your reaction to being asked to consider each one. It would not be possible to arrange them in a scale, because different individuals have different inclinations, and repulsions, and a scale based on social values would produce a rather strange arrangement; it is statistically provable, for example, that more people have slept with neighbors' wives or husbands than have sold their possessions to give to the poor.

There is nothing in this list that has not been done. I haven't asked you to consider "going to Mars" or "becoming twenty feet tall." There is probably also nothing in the list you haven't thought of, at least fleetingly or frivolously. If you rejected it without deliberation on the ground that it was silly or revolting or "unthinkable," it may be that you never really rejected it—you just shoved it down out of sight.

My point is that freedom of thought requires abandoning the notion that *contemplating* any act is silly or revolting. If you know your Uncle Louie plans to leave you a hundred thousand dollars when he departs this life, you can't help knowing that the sooner he leaves, the sooner you'll have your hands on it. That doesn't mean there might not be good reasons for not killing him. The best reason would be if you love the old guy and want him to enjoy life as long as he can. If this is not the case, then there is a second-best reason for not bumping him off. Even if you don't love him, you respect his right to stay alive as equal to yours. And third, if this is not the case, there is yet another excellent reason for deciding against any move to erase him: It is very unlikely it could be done without eventual discovery—it wouldn't be worth it. If none of these three reasons has any meaning at all to you, you may already have a plan. You are sick, emotionally and mentally, and my advice at this point is not to you but to Uncle Louie: Get yourself a food taster, or have your lawyers send notice to your heirs that you'll give them their inheritance before you go and that if death catches you unawares, the whole bundle goes to a cat hospital.

Everyone should be allowed and encouraged to consider any idea or action that crosses his mind on its merits, without the prejudice of infantile taboos. Only then is a free and responsible choice made. A society seeking stability through the suppression of such mental activity risks its morality resting on a foundation of fear and obedience rather than responsibility and caring. No amount of police could sustain order in a society based on the first.

I believe the practice of what I call oblique volition develops and gives direction to self-motivation. I believe that small beginnings are not useless. In my personal experience I have been surprised by the results of but tiny efforts of this kind.

You do not fashion yourself into a completely mature person and then start behaving maturely. You begin by trying to behave maturely. You try to get a foothold on this steep path by using some energy to acquire a technique for directing the vital drive of self-reconstruction. Some of this effort can profitably employ oblique volition, no matter how foolish or fruitless it may seem at first. Get up and try the door of the dungeon. *Try* the safe deposit lock, even if you know you lack half the keys.

### [3]

There are three kinds of oblique volition: one involving conscious choice of suitable targets peripheral to the central problem, another involving random targets not necessarily related to the central problem, and a third involving nonaction: simply turning your back on the problem and doing nothing at all about it. This last seems paradoxical, but there are special instances when the best treatment of an emotional problem is to do nothing about it.

Here is an example of oblique volition involving a suitable peripheral target related to the central problem.

You have trouble "speaking your mind," and you go away from encounters wishing you'd said such-and-such. If this is a firmly entrenched problem in your life, you may already have discovered that merely telling yourself "not to be that way" has done no good at all. But you can quit trying to push against the main problem and select a peripheral target. For example, decide in advance what you should say to the person you have trouble expressing yourself to, and write it down, as plainly and concisely as possible; send it to him as a memo. It gets the job done, and you may find he will not be angry or crushed or misunderstanding, or whatever you feared in the way of reaction. If he wonders out loud why you wrote it down instead of just telling him, tell him the truth: that you would have difficulty voicing it.

Why you can't say it doesn't matter. Not even to you. A psychiatrist might be able to find a reason—a simple one, or very complicated—but you are not a psychiatrist. Your problem is getting the car out of the ditch, not finding out how it got there. If real tries to correct your problem seem to be getting you nowhere and it's serious enough to hamper your effectiveness or happiness, let a psychiatrist have a crack at it. But trying to help yourself could do two things: (1) it might effect the correction, proving that you didn't need professional help, and (2) the effort itself will have done a lot of the doctor's work, saving time and money and enhancing the chances of a successful outcome.

If you find after a few times that reactions are not as violent as expected, try then to voice your thoughts without undue caution. Even if it seems tactless or cruel or hostile, if it is necessary and honest, say it and let the chips fall where they may. You may find that the habit of carrying over your memo-writing pattern into spontaneous speech has paid off.

A second, less specific, use of oblique volition comes into play when no suitable peripheral targets present themselves. Here the technique is to do almost anything other than attack the central problem, *but to do something*. An example: You have trouble making decisions. You notice that your indecision has the effect of letting fate decide most things. Things left undecided will eventually resolve themselves one way or another, but fate's decisions are sometimes the least desirable of all alternatives. Nevertheless, quit trying to force yourself to "make" decisions in those areas that give you trouble. *And quit worrying about it.* Instead, start making decisive changes in little things, things that don't matter. Don't try to relate them to decisions. Your choices can be capricious. If you normally brush your teeth in the morning before showering, reverse the order. Skip a meal. Prepare or order and eat some food you have always disliked. Don't use these examples; make up your own. If this all seems silly and unrewarding and you believe that it can't possibly solve your big problem, keep in mind that you are absolutely right. As long as you regard the technique as silly and unrewarding, you will defeat it from the outset. You will probably not even try it, thus proving your point. "This can't possibly work" is a self-fulfilling prophecy when applied to any motivational problem.

But the technique of rut-busting—getting yourself out of a rut by starting with little, unrelated acts—can work wonders in overcoming big problems.

A farmer wanted to get rid of a grove of trees in order to plow and plant the land. Unskilled in wood cutting, he knew he couldn't do it himself. But he could try cutting bushes and small trees at the edge. He began to get the hang of it after a while, and tried his hand at larger trees. He kept practicing for months until he realized he was probably skilled enough to tackle the grove. But the grove was gone. He'd used it up in practice.

The third and subtlest use of oblique volition had to do with not doing anything at all. It is at the same time the easiest and the most difficult action conceivable, because it is *nonaction*.

If a magical jinni appeared and offered you a million dollars if you could "not think of turtles for one minute," could you do it? Of course not. It is beyond the power of the mind to concentrate on not giving attention to something. But this is closely related to the following suggestion for the nonaction technique of solving a problem.

Let us suppose your problem is insomnia, because you worry a lot: either a specific worry or nameless floating fears that keep you awake when you need rest and sleep. You have tried such things as counting sheep, and want to avoid excessive reliance on sleeping pills, but nothing has really worked, and you are at your wits' end (which means literally that all your knowledge, or reasoning power, brought to bear on your problem has failed to resolve it). Let us define "worry" not as constructive concern that leads to careful consideration of alternatives and choice among them, but as the rejection of all alternatives and the continual return to the same starting point, going through the cycle again and again. This cycle needs breaking up. No frontal attack on the problem has availed—such as attempting to take your mind off it by conscious efforts at relaxation; no related peripheral target for an oblique move proved effective—such as going to the gym or walking to work to get physically tired; and no capricious unrelated moves such as taking up a new hobby, or rearranging the furniture, or eating persimmons (which you detest), or buying your wife a surprise gift (which only made her suspect that you had a guilty conscience about something) has done any good. You still lie in bed, tired but not sleepy, worried but not moving toward a solution of the problem causing the worry. So you say to yourself, "There is apparently nothing I can do."

And in that statement is the key to solving the problem.

Do *nothing* about it.

But how do you "do nothing" about the fact that every night you lie in bed not sleeping?

First, recognize that you are concerned because you were brought up to believe that certain hours should be spent awake and certain hours sleeping, and you must force yourself into this mold.

Now, shift the emphasis slightly so that instead of "do *nothing* about it," the admonition reads, "do nothing about *it*." If when you go to bed you are sleepy, sleep. If you are not sleepy, get up, get dressed, and do something else. You have letters to write, books to read, projects to complete in the basement workshop. Night is a time of great industry. There are all-night movies, some of them worth seeing; there are late late television shows. Yes, but, you point out, you are tired and will be forcing yourself. Are you not forcing yourself at work in the daytime after a sleepless night? Why should your job have a monopoly on forcing yourself? If you go sleepless long enough you may have to knock off work, for sick leave—and if you've lost enough sleep, you will indeed be sick.

The important thing is not to lie in bed at night worrying about not getting enough sleep, on top of everything else. Give your attention to anything else at any time you are sleepless, day or night. If this results in turning night into day, but breaks up the deadlock and solves the problem, then the weird schedule will prove temporary. You may lose less time at work than if you broke down and had to be hospitalized. Turn your back on the problem of sleeplessness and give your undivided attention to anything else, and you will be "not thinking of turtles." You are also very likely to get to sleep and get back to a practical schedule sooner than you had thought possible.

# CHAPTER VI

## Attitudes

[1]

A happy person is not a person in a certain set of circumstances, but rather a person with a certain set of attitudes.

John has a broken back, is going deeper into debt every day in the hospital, and has just learned that his family narrowly escaped injury in a fire that damaged the recreation room and dining alcove of his small home.

Pete has a large home, is on the eve of a vacation, has just received the results of an insurance examination that pronounced him in perfect health, and as one result of a recent promotion and increase in income has just told his wife she can have the family car as her very own, since he will now purchase the sports car he wanted.

It's possible that both these men are unhappy. And it's possible that they both are happy. To illustrate a point, however, let us assume that John, lying in his hospital bed, is pleased with his progress, noting that each day he has less pain. He has plans for a way to consolidate his debts through a loan; he feels a deep gratitude that his family was helped to safety during the fire by firemen who prevented the complete destruction of his home, and has talked by phone with his insurance man about how he intends to use the insurance money to do over those two rooms. John enjoys do-it-yourself projects and intends to absorb labor costs by paneling the rooms himself. He looks forward to getting out of the hospital, but enjoys sleeping, eating, reading, and thinking.

On the other hand, Pete, sitting on his terrace, worries about his landscaping looking less manicured than his neighbor's. His gardener has quit, and he hasn't been able to locate another. He is afraid of losing status in the neighborhood by appearing to be unable to afford a gardener, so he doesn't do any of the work himself, even though he would like to, since he enjoys gardening. He wanted to go to Nassau, but they are going to Sweden because that was the choice of his wife, with whom he is bored. He does not enjoy reading or eating, sleeps poorly, and looks forward to getting back from Sweden.

The point is that happiness, and in a sense wealth, are rooted in attitudes that are relatively independent of material means; further, these attitudes are characteristic of a mature outlook on life, an outlook that is desirable and attainable for many people regardless of age or current level of maturity. Those who believe that a great amount of money is a responsibility they could bear up under easily are not necessarily wrong. With the appropriate attitude, wealth, even the sudden unearned acquisition of it, need not be destructive. And neither grinding poverty nor the loss of material possessions can be viewed as conducive to developing a state of happiness. Aristotle believed that a degree of wealth was necessary to happiness. The virtues of poverty may have been overstressed by an age in which religious orders were founded on self-denial. Most people will not fall into great wealth, earned or unearned, so that problem is largely academic. The real problem is how to acquire or build a set of attitudes that will allow and encourage maturing (as a continuing process) that in turn will prove a source of happiness fairly independent of external circumstances of wealth and poverty, fortune and misfortune.

It is almost impossible to name these attitudes, because what we actually name are the *results* of attitudes. An attitude is like a concept of "self" or "soul," because naming forces a "thing" concept, and "soul" and "self" are not "things" in the ordinary sense. Neither is attitude. So the following attitudes are named with adjectives.

1. The *zestful attitude*. Regarding the world and its particulars as fresh. The world cannot be stale. Only the manner of viewing it stagnates. The subtle shift from an attitude of wonder and zest to one that is as Shakespeare described it in Hamlet, "weary, stale, flat and unprofitable" can come from prolonged overconcern for a facet of personal security, causing too much attention to be given to that one concern and a measuring of all other things in the light of how "useful" they may be in serving the problem. A clue is to be found in the word "unprofitable," as used in the Shakespeare quote. A zestful attitude requires freedom from marketplace evaluating of all encountered phenomena.

2. The *expansive attitude*. Participating in extrapersonal processes and feelings. This again is part of "getting outside yourself." The social, the empathetic and affective outlooks characterize the expansive attitude. It requires considerable excursion outside the ego shell and in higher planes of maturity, a sort of dismantling of the ego.

3. The *timeless attitude*. Focusing on the moment and shedding the past and the future. This does not, of course, mean abolishing memory (past) or anticipation and planning (future). It means a proper use of those faculties in which memory can be drawn on or savored without constituting a refuge from the uncertainties of the present moment, and with which the future can be provided for and enjoyed in anticipation without being a place to escape from a continuously irritating present. It is undue emphasis on the past and future that gives them the false light of being greater realities than the present. A timeless attitude toward the "now" makes the past exist only in memory and the future no more than a vast number of possibilities with varying probabilities—both past and future being useful, but not real in the sense that life at the present moment is real. This is childlike,

in that the child, having a smaller store of memories, and less responsibility for planning than the grownup, is better able to focus on the "now." The grownup has more to remember and more responsibility for the future. If the attitude he maintains is one of compulsively dwelling on the remembered pleasures and pains of past experiences, and compulsively regarding the future with overprudence, he will retreat from the present. This is one of the characteristics of an immature adult. If, on the other hand, his attitude enables him to see the past as real only to the extent that it provides for a rational use of memory for learning, and the future as real only for calculating probabilities and formulating plans, he is mature. In this attitude the more memory he accumulates, the more he has learned, the more techniques he has acquired, and the less he need fear the present moment. Also, the more skill he develops in dealing with the future, the less concerned he will be with how vulnerable he is to the present moment; hence the more childlike he can be in his openness to the present.

4. The *active attitude*. Initiating rather than merely reacting. The active attitude is a jewel in a setting made up of vulnerability, internal organization, and security in the face of continuing threat. Among the things a maturing individual has learned is that the pain of responsibility and commitment is tolerable. A desperate need to avoid all pain in life is a serious block to action. It is also a hopeless goal. The active attitude of the mature human reflects a highly efficient and stable internal organization—he is confident it won't be overthrown easily, and it is capable of handling disturbing information with maximum learning and minimum damage. This attitude harbors no illusions of invulnerability, but neither is it overfearful of being destroyed by an experiment or error. We are tougher than we think. Most people (since most people are immature) desire invulnerability rather than life. Since there is no invulerable condition for the human, the wish is both vain and pathetic. The active attitude says, "If I am going to suffer, let it be because of my actions." Pursuing this policy teaches two things: (a) The

pain is bearable; (b) modes of acting, refined by experience, allow increased scope of action without increase of pain.

The attitude of *reaction*, on the other hand, teaches these two things: (a) Pain is unavoidable anyway, no matter how skillful the pirouetting away from blows; (b) a course of life set by the random buffetings of a capricious universe is not only in itself painful, it is also empty. This emptiness is the only death worthy of our fear.

5. The *generic attitude*. Having a sense of relation to the entire universe. This is an attitude characteristic of one who has a unifying philosophy of life. It is in this sense a religious sentiment. It is appropriate to a mature personality because it "lays itself open to all facts, to all values, and disvalues, and claims to have the clue to their theoretical and practical inclusion in a frame of life."\* One with this attitude believes that his life is oriented and committed to "what he regards as permanent or central in the nature of things," as Allport puts it.

We see in this, more than in any other attitude, the characteristic of self as more than individual, since it requires both feeding and being fed by the "external" world. It *is*, in a sense, the external world.

These are the attitudes. How do we assimilate or develop them? How do we help someone with blue eyes to have brown eyes if that's what he says he needs to be happy? What he really wants, and it is a reasonable desire, is to move from unhappiness to happiness. It may be impossible to change the color of his eyes, but not necessarily impossible to help him abandon the belief that he must change it in order to be happy.

He is unhappy, he says, because his eyes are not the color he desires them to be. The "because" clause of a statement may be true and yet the whole be false.

In the nineteenth century people thought that air travel between the United States and Europe would remain forever im-

\* Gordon Allport, *The Individual and His Religion* (New York: Macmillan, 1950), p. 54.

possible because the hot-air balloon could not span the Atlantic Ocean. The second part of this—the "because" clause—is true, but the first part is false.

There is a Zen parable that tells of a fool who went searching for fire with a lighted lantern. "Had he known the nature of fire, he could have cooked his rice much sooner." We want happiness, peace, an end to suffering. The specifics we deem essential to these things are often in error, and the pursuit of them can stand in the way of the real goal.

One thing that keeps us from knowing what we can do is not knowing really what we cannot do. Two basic kinds of limitations form boundaries to human actions, and the two are often confused. One is general, the other personal. One is a set of limitations delineated by general size, strength, longevity, intellect, endurance, speed of reflexes, sexual capability, memory, resistance to disease, etc. The boundaries are hazy. But in the main we all form, with reasonable and workable accuracy, an idea of what the practical limits are for masses of people, and what an average is. This is the first basic type of human limitation. A healthy person accepts these limitations. He may seek to expand his accomplishments, to crowd or cross the boundaries of human limits, but he realistically assesses his chances of accomplishing each goal set, and his desires are scaled to the probability of attainment. It's healthy to desire and save toward getting a new record player or pair of skis or a house, but it's unrealistic and unhealthy to nurse a prolonged thirst to build and maintain a four-hundred-foot yacht, or to own and rule a small country. It would be very unhealthy to develop any real desire to grow to a height of thirty feet or to be able to lift a freight locomotive.

Healthy living requires a sound knowledge not only of these limits and averages, but a realistic idea of where each of our own personal powers lies in its respective spectrum. This is the second basic type of limitation: personal limitation. You may be smaller than the average adult human of your sex but have muscular strength well above what you have observed to be average in your age group. If you were first in your class and made

Phi Beta Kappa, you may correctly conclude you have superior intellect and learning ability. All of these spectra constitute a multidimensional continuum in which you fit with a certain shape. Psychologists say that the degree to which your self-portrait coincides with your real shape in this continuum is an indication of your ability to be "realistic" about yourself.

Keep in mind that your "real" shape in this continuum is not clearly discernible, even to intimates. Some facets are immediately apparent, such as physical size, but many things are matters of subjective judgment, many things require long-term knowledge of the individual, and many things can be camouflaged or hidden by the individual. Beauty, for example, is somewhat subjective. How many times have you met someone who struck you as ordinary-looking, perhaps even plain, and found as you got better acquainted that the person began to look beautiful? Conversely, how many conventionally "good-looking" people later seemed plain or even homely when you discovered in them an objectionable personality?

Intellect is not easy to assess quickly. It's difficult to get more than a rough idea of an individual's intellect in one meeting. Even formal tests are not totally sound. Some "flashy" people seem brilliant but are not really intelligent, and some very intelligent people may be shy or plodding in conversation. A person who is highly articulate and able to "showcase" his abilities with skill may persuade newcomers for a short time that he is more intelligent than is actually the case. A person may hide thoughtlessness successfully for a time by being solicitous and attentive. He may be using the "this-will-convince-them-I'm-a-hell-of-a-nice-fellow" technique.

If the individual is conscious of some lack in himself and constantly needs to create an impression inconsistent with what he believes himself to be, he is in mild trouble. Emotionally he feels he can't be accepted on the basis of what he really is.

On the other hand, he may not be conscious of a lack in himself, feeling rather that the world is stupid or perverse in not accepting him, thus forcing him to present what he feels is his true self with heavy emphasis.

This attitude never has the desired effect. Boasting and posturing, or more subtle variations of these habits, are designed to win some kind of acceptance, but instead create an opposite effect, and should be abandoned. When they persist, they are explained as "compulsive." The person who employs these techniques is said to operate on an infantile level and fails at least in this area to learn or accomplish. If we leave the explanation at that, it seems that some emotional inadequacy merely causes the person to fail in his quest for acceptance. There is an interpretation of psychological theory, however, that goes much deeper in explaining this phenomenon and that shows that the habit is not productive of failure but of a type of success, and explains its persistence: Why would a good, functioning, rational mind persist in a habit that does not produce the effect it appears to desire? The answer lies in examination of what a person may appear to desire and what he may really desire. His boasting and posturing may not be devices for gaining acceptance at all, but rather for preventing acceptance. A sound intellect can serve a stunted emotional makeup, and a sound intellect knows that acceptance will not come from others unless the real person is presented. It knows also the inadequacies of the real person it works for and knows that that person does not want to be accepted as having inadequacies. So when the emotional side calls for protection against this painful possibility and at the same time demands protection from the anxiety that comes with nonacceptance, the intellect is up against a dilemma: "Do something," it is told, "to shield me from this anxiety of not being accepted by my fellows, but don't let them really accept me, because in doing so they will know what I am really like. And if they find out what I am really like, I am apt to have to face it myself, and I don't have the stomach for it."

Sound Intellect might reply: "This is not easy, particularly since you hamper and fetter me. But if you have to have a solution right away, I can suggest a way out for each situation. It won't really solve the main problem, but it is comfortable." And if Sound Intellect has a nodding acquaintance with psychoanalytic theory, it might add: "I suggest you put me to work devising actions that might change what you are really like so you will eventually have no need of all these gymnastics."

Warped Emotion answers: "Not on your life. I have access to your thoughts, and some of them are quite frightening. I don't want to hear them. Just tell me what you've come up with to let me go through the motions of being accepted without really having that happen. And if I have to face any failure because of the paradoxical nature of this command, fix up a rationale that puts the blame on the world. There's solid comfort in that. It can't be my fault."

Sound Intellect: O.K. But I'll be working overtime. Here's what we do: Try to convince everybody that you're superior on every count. Hammer them on the head with it. They won't buy it, but you will. That way you won't feel anxious, and there's no chance of real acceptance by anyone unless maybe your mother, but—

Warped Emotion: She's your mother too.

Sound Intellect: Intellect has no mother.

Warped Emotion: Anyway, she never accepted either of us.

Sound Intellect: Thank God it doesn't bother me. It shouldn't matter to you.

Warped Emotion: I don't want to talk about it.

Sound Intellect: You see how I'm hampered and fettered? Anyway, let me know if you want a better plan. A long-range one. It involves some real discomfort for a while, but you'd thank me in the end.

An important consideration in the health and maturity of the individual is whether any camouflage he employs is (1) merely acceding to the protocol of his culture, to be indulged perfunctorily and then dropped; (2) an ongoing pattern needed to make corrections in the way others are likely to see him, or (3) distortions aimed at defending a false image of himself *for* himself as well as others.

The first case is linked to what we call manners. An immature person may feel he "must" go through these rituals, or he may be unaware that they are rituals. A somewhat more mature person knows the nature of the moves but is emancipated from any necessity of following them—he may, for a variety of reasons, drop the pretense and be seen to lack politeness. A still more mature human being will resume most of the ritual, not harboring any illusions about the game nature of etiquette, but neither feeling any necessity to display his emancipation from it. He will abrogate a custom, not to rebel, but only if it cuts across some line of his inner morality. For example, he might shake hands and say, "How do you do" to be polite, or he might even indulge the hypocrisy of a small lie in saying "Nice to have met you" to someone whom it was not nice to have met, but here he is not anxious to please, and he would not have "being agreeable" as a prime goal. In things that matter to him he will say what he thinks and do as he pleases.

[2]

The second case (an ongoing pattern employed to make corrections in the way others are likely to see us) is an inability to be ourselves. This is usually because we don't quite like ourselves as we are, and we reason that others are not going to accept us unless we doctor the image slightly. If this is a mild disorder, not affecting the whole personality but only certain aspects of it, and if, further, there is not a deep need to keep those aspects as they are and deal with other people by a permanent technique of distorting the presentation of self, there is a chance they will prove easily correctable. Three examples of the same apparent disorder may serve to show different levels of trouble. James and Roger and Doug were three young men with a common trait. They were loud and tended to dominate conversations. James was aware that people had mentioned this to him and realized they might be right. He embarked on a plan of self-improvement, including a personality course. By practicing restraint, he learned that he was better accepted after a while and his new mode of behavior gradually required less effort and eventually became habit.

Roger's case was a little different. Here also, friends mentioned to him his tendency to dominate conversations, and on each occasion he would withdraw, dampened and hurt for a while, sometimes really trying to avoid offending by not dominating the conversation or by softening his tone. But his sincerity was each time aimed at correcting the situation at hand, rather than correcting himself, and it was a long time before he decided to try some self-improvement. When he finally did, enrolling as James had done in a personality course, he tried for a time to acquire a technique that would correct what he now accepted as a flaw, but he found it too frustrating and didn't finish the course. He mellowed some over the years, but always faced the alternatives of being comfortable, but loud and objectionable, or accepted but throttled and frustrated.

Doug's case is still different. "Friends" who made bold to mention his objectionable quality immediately became enemies, and he was grieved that people he had respected could fall so low. Where both James and Roger had felt (mistakenly) that they were insignificant and smaller than average in some basic way, and that to compensate for it and gain attention it was necessary to force (to amplify an inadequate voice), Doug was not conscious of any inadequacy on his part. He successfully kept ideas of self-inferiority out of his conscious thought by projecting an idea of inferiority on everything else: The inadequacy was that of a world that failed to accept him. Proof of this lay all around. Didn't people criticize him instead of praising him? Didn't friends prove false in the end by turning into critics? The world was a treacherous place, and everyone he knew fell short. Over the years Doug's frustrations built. It is hard for a paragon to make his home among the lowly. The world got worse, and more and more people turned on him. This situation was not imaginary, for the more objectionable he became, the less accepted he was. The final vindication of the paranoid outlook is that the world *does* at last turn against the paranoid personality. Then he can say, "I told you so."

One of the saddest aspects of a situation like Doug's is that it is so resistant to forces inside or out that might correct it. A man like this must suffer a lot. He might even get glimpses of the real nature of his problem. But what he sees may be so painful that it merely produces a hasty retreat into the fantasy that at once both gives comfort and prolongs the difficulty. In moments of insight Doug could have sought help through therapy. He would have been in for a lot of pain. But if he stuck with it (even if initially only to see how wrong or treacherous the psychiatrist was), and if he'd chosen a good, skilled doctor, there is a chance he'd have been able to make real improvement in himself, and life a lot easier for him and those around him.

So James's case was a slight personality flaw, not much more than a mannerism that had gotten out of hand, and the correction was spontaneous in that disapproval of his behavior was "in the air" much as spores or stray neutrons are everywhere, and he seized and acted on that criticism.

Roger's situation showed the same kind of flaw in his perception of himself, but was deeper and involved more discomfort in taking corrective action. And so he abandoned a sincere effort to correct himself. The pain of continuing might have been much less than he anticipated.

Doug's case is a real tragedy. Hurt deeply enough to be blinded to the true nature of the disorder, he was in a spiral that lacked any positive feedback and would have failed to stabilize at any level. Frustration gave rise to an even less realistic attitude, and a diminishing contact with reality bred more and more frustration.

Still, the force that generates insight is operative in anyone who is alive. It is still possible to rise up from the dungeon floor and walk out. It's still possible to accept painful limitations and to act *in a new direction*. If all else has failed and the situation is desperate and the world is a very unhappy place, it is possible to try the acute pain of facing for a moment the possibility that it's you and not the world that is off-base. Action based on this (of course, preposterous) assumption will be irrational nonsense unrelated to the problem, but since frontal attacks have failed, what is there to lose in an oblique action? It is not so important whether your appraisal or diagnosis is accurate *as that you make one and act on it*. Action in the case of oblique volition is more important than understanding.

If you are troubled, how should you be advised? Advice is easy to give, and so it comes from everywhere. The attitude of the advised may be more important than the content of the advice. Here is mine.

1. Review your limitations. First consider those limitations common to all humans, and then make an assessment of those limitations you feel are peculiar to you. Correctness in this effort is not as important as the effort to be as honest as possible.

2. Accept the idea, if only as a working hypothesis, that you can correct the trouble. Remember that a limitation is not necessarily a trouble. If you are only four feet tall and it doesn't bother you, you have nothing to correct. If you can't handle alcohol and have quit drinking, you are functioning within your limitations. The best thing about the way the world is made is that situations and conditions you really can't change are not real causes of emotional unhappiness or pain. And all real causes of unhappiness or pain stemming from emotional factors are within your power to abolish. Put another way, the world is neither good nor bad, pain or pleasure, moral or immoral, useful or useless. It is only wonderful. All these values come from the way the fabric of our individuality is stretched and contoured on the world. Stretch one corner excessively and it's painful. You have created the pain by insisting that you have more fabric in that area than you actually possess—by exceeding some limitation. Stretched enough to create debilitating pain, it is a neurosis. Stretched far enough to rip, it is a psychosis.

3. Be suspicious of any unhappiness you really feel comes from outside yourself. If your enemies are many, and your friends prove false by criticizing you, and the world seems generally hostile,

be very suspicious, not of them, but of your idea of where the cause of unhappiness lies. However outlandish or painful it may be to consider that the trouble is inside you *and to act on that assumption*, you are free to try considering it and acting on it. If the world can't be manipulated and changed by you, give the other a try. The real cause of any emotional unhappiness is within your power to deal with, and since it is clearly not in your power to change the world, try the other.

4. If nothing seems to avail in direct confrontation with the problem, try acting obliquely. Stab around the periphery of the difficulty for a while. The reason this sometimes works is because it brings on action instead of theorizing—it allows spontaneity. Often directly attacking the central problem is too painful to allow real action on it. Until the mechanism of motivation is fired up and running it can't be brought to bear on the problem. Take the car out of gear and get the motor running in idle; it may never start while it's in gear. This is parallel to "sleeping on the problem" or taking a vacation before an arduous project. A mountain man, trapper and guide, once gave this advice for any solitary scout in a "fix": "Sit down on a stump or log, fill a pipe, and smoke it to the bottom before doing anything." This procedure reduces the danger of panicking and lets the mind idle through the problem instead of forcing it.

It's important to emphasize that my advice concerns only emotionally rooted problems. There are real external, physical, political, and social problems in the world. There are real auto accidents, real injustices, real persecutions. A sensitive person with a strong sense of justice should not be expected to "adjust" to a society that mounts injustices. "To be a mature *adult* is to be psychologically healthy; to be a psychologically healthy adult is to be mature—though in both cases, such a person is not necessarily normal or perfectly adjusted to his society."† He may suffer, and

† Douglas Heath, *Explorations of Maturity* (New York: Appleton-Century-Crofts, 1965), p. 4.

his suffering is not because he is emotionally ill. Would one have told a Jew in Hitler's Germany to be suspicious not of his persecutors but of some emotional warp on his part? One wouldn't have.

# CHAPTER VII

## *Development of Attitudes—"The Sausage Machine"*

### [1]

What action, oblique or otherwise, can the individual take in order to adopt the five attitudes listed in the previous chapter as both characteristic of and conducive to maturity?

The way to a zestful attitude is not to make the world more fresh, but to make ourselves less stale. Bertrand Russell, in his excellent book *The Conquest of Happiness*, writes, "There were once upon a time two sausage machines exquisitely constructed for the purpose of turning pig into the most delicious sausages. One of these retained his zest for pig and produced sausages innumerable; the other said: 'What is pig to me? My own works are far more interesting and wonderful than any pig.' He refused pig and set to work to study his inside. When bereft of its natural food, his inside ceased to function, and the more he studied it the more empty and foolish it seemed to him to be. All the exquisite apparatus by which the delicious transformation had hitherto been made stood still, and he was at a loss to guess what it was capable of doing. This second sausage machine was like a man who has lost his zest, while the first was like a man who has retained it.*

* Bertrand Russell, *The Conquest of Happiness* (New York: Liveright, 1971), p. 77.

Most advice aimed at retaining or developing zest in living boils down to an admonition to abandon preoccupation with self. The freshness of the world is limitless; to be preoccupied with oneself offers a very limited field of attention. It goes stale in a hurry.

An actor was once asked, after seven hundred performances in the same play, if it was stale to him. He said, "When I step onstage I'm conscious of an audience for whom the performance is opening night. They've never seen the play before. Each night there is a fresh audience, and the seven hundredth performance is just as new as the first. If I thought of myself, the play would have been stale by the tenth performance."

Perhaps it requires a great deal of security—a great deal of confidence in one's artistic technique—to keep an audience in mind while acting a role. Inner security is necessary to living in this manner—i.e., keeping other people and things in mind in everything we do. It is necessary to shed undue concern about ourselves, physical and emotional, in order to turn the attention outward. To do this we must establish a sense of security, and establish a constant increase in its development. For this it is necessary to mature sufficiently to allocate an appropriate proportion of attention to the self and give the rest to the world.

So we have come around a giant circle that starts with the advice to "be mature" and ends with the same advice.

I've noticed this about so many inspirational and self-help books. The real question all along is, "How do I enter the circle? At what point and by what means can I get a grip on the problem and start working on it?" Readers have a right to say, "I know all that. I know I should develop more inner security. I know I need to be more mature. But how do I go about doing it?"

It seems here that we have a case of the third type of oblique volition. Paradoxically, the inner sense of security must be established by a type of "nonaction" that results in making us less secure. To explain this let me advance two techniques. The first I call the "running start" and the second "out on a limb." The "running start" involves a deliberate move away from the goal of establishing zest, and the "out on a limb" involves a commitment equivalent to sawing the limb off.

Reactivating the jaded, inspiring the uninspired, installing zest in the unzestful—here more than in any undertaking I know is futility. More than anything else, the impossibility of manipulation from outside is manifest. Let's imagine a man with flaccid muscles whose need is to exercise. Can we "exercise" him? Would the job be done by seizing his arms and legs and moving them through calisthenic routines? Our best hope is to do something to make him want to move his limbs himself and to stay with it long enough so that the exercise will show itself to be tolerable, useful, and at last pleasurable. He must come to these truths himself.

The problem with the jaded—those with flabby emotional muscles—is that of all boring things in the whole boring world, advice not to be bored is the most boring. So there are 2½ strikes on anyone who embarks on a project of "unboring" someone else. Nothing is more repulsive to the eyes of ennui than the bounding enthusiasm of those around him. This may explain why bored people seek the company of other bored people.

It is not the purpose of this book to try to alter the state of anyone whose attitude of boredom is so important to him that he clings to it with desperation. These words are intended only for those who would like to revive in themselves something they remember from an earlier time—those who believe it might *not* be the world that has gone stale, those who are willing to consider that there might be some action they could take to bring about this change, but who have either not yet tried, or have tried and failed.

Among possible methods of reviving zest *through advice*, we will not find anything in the way of external action. It must come from inside. Short of a complete collapse of the will to live, there is always a hope or a desire for positive action struggling to get out from under a layer of obstructing material. The volition of those who want to save themselves from stultifying boredom should be directed to removing obstructions rather than forcing attention. This is painful but essential. Urban renewal calls for some housewrecking at the beginning. Eduard von Hartman tells us in *Philosophy of the Unconscious* that many lower forms of life are able to reject injured or threatened limbs voluntarily as a first step in reconstruction. Then they grow new limbs. Although Freud formulated a hypothesis of a death instinct (primary impulses of destructiveness turned inward), Karl Menninger says, ". . . there is always a degree of spontaneous self-*reconstruction* along with the self-destruction."† To reinforce this drive to self-reconstruction—and tip the scales, however slightly, in the direction of the will to live—is the dedication of the psychiatrist and the hope of all who write and read "advice." Possibly the active ingredient in all such advice is this hope, this desire to acquire and share a margin on the side of the will to live. "The private citizen no less than the psychiatrist and the social worker may, by dint of the simple expedients of an encouraging smile, a sympathetic inquiry, a patient audience to an outpouring of trouble, lift burdens of depression, diminish the woes of voluntary or involuntary martyrdom and frustrate the urge toward self-destructiveness of many a sufferer," says Menninger.

For the zestless person who would like to recapture his zest, as a first action I'd like to suggest what I call the "running start." To jump over a wide ditch you may have to back up a few feet, actually going away from your goal, which is the other side of the ditch. My suggestion is to seek things and situations that are actually more boring than the ordinary dull facets of your existence. Stop seeking things that might interest you and look instead for things that are duller than usual. Sit through a mediocre theater performance, or movie, or TV program. Read through a small-town newspaper. "Take a dullard to lunch," and listen carefully to everything he says. (You might be in for the shock of finding he is employing the same technique in having lunch with you.)

I remember driving through the state of Kansas when it was

† Karl Menninger, *Man Against Himself* (New York: Harcourt, Brace, 1938), p. 367.

112° F. Through the open windows of the car poured air that seemed right out of a blast furnace. Since it seemed that the outside air was doing nothing to cool the inside of the car, I rolled the windows up. In the stifling heat, perspiration began to soak through my shirt. When I opened the windows I found the warm air dry enough to evaporate the moisture thus collected, and for a few minutes I cooled off. It seemed to me that the suffering I underwent in that momentary increase in temperature was more than offset by the subsequent cooling.

This asceticism is, it's true, like banging your head against the wall because it feels good when you stop, but it can sometimes break the kind of deadlock that makes the whole world dull to you.

If the "running start" ploy doesn't work for you, there are other things to try. Look for excitement—but the right kind. An "insatiable thirst for excitement" usually means seeking the wrong kind of excitement. Courting physical danger, excessive gambling, and careless and reckless driving have more than a hint of self-destructiveness: They may provide momentary diversion from the boredom of life, but they are not the kind of activities that provide any remedial or healing effect.

But there is a kind of excitement within the grasp of anyone, which carries more corrective power: This is what I call "out on a limb." Put yourself into a situation where you are hungry for a while. Not merely the ascetic exercise of skipping a meal, but the kind of situation in which you will need all your skill to figure where your next meal is coming from. This can be done simply by setting out in a wilderness with a gun, matches, a hand ax, and a skinning knife and going far enough that you must stay overnight, devising shelter and getting food. It might be uncomfortable, but it won't be boring. Remember, it is not discomfort you seek to escape, but boredom. And if the limb you have put yourself out on is one in which most of your energies are occupied in satisfying your elementary physical needs, the zest for living will return.

The pain of a right-angle turn in life, even one self-imposed, can evolve, through discomfort, to zest.

Boredom can always be escaped. The honest statement of the problem is that we want to escape it without sacrificing the comforts and surfeits that are themselves at the root of our ennui. Perhaps this is why this very real type of suffering elicits so little sympathy.

To review, the "running start" technique can, in some instances, break a deadlock and open the way to a cure for boredom. But it is, after all, asceticism; and ascetic gestures from which there is immediate possible retreat are not the same and not as powerful as actions that represent irrevocable commitments. Taking a real plunge like quitting your job or getting rid of possessions may court discomfort, but it ends boredom. All zest has its roots in discomfort of some kind. Hunger is, indeed, the best sauce.

Recapture your zest, and you've removed another obstacle to maturing.

[2]

The expansive attitude overlaps the zestful. Although getting outside yourself is a necessary step to zestful living, it is part of the very essence of the expansive attitude. The newborn human brings many processes into the world with him. Beneath his consciousness are such organic skills as utilization of nutrition (post-digestive); cell division and differentiation; a blood pump, formed and working; and a functioning network of sensory and motor nerves coupled to muscles that have been given a few brief trial runs before birth. But whole systems are thrust into action at launching time or soon after that have developed with no trial use, among them lungs and eyes and digestive apparatus. The sudden shift from potential to kinetic would make it seem to him that this new place he has arrived at is an inferno (except that he brings no concept of an inferno with him). He is intensely aware.

His mind is a great blank territory for the registering of experiences received in their purest form, uncluttered with labels, unencrusted with the barnacles of past impression or the prejudices of cultural conditioning. There is no past. He is starting *now*. And his mind is so purely virginal that he is in a sense identical with the awareness of all that's going on within and without. He has not as yet adopted the convention that his skin forms a boundary that separates "him" from the rest of the universe, nor the emotional parallel that will come with the formation of an idea of ego that will tend to *isolate* him from the rest of the world.

His education is about to begin. He is about to start learning names and games and do's and don'ts and musts and oughts and goods and bads—all useful for relating to other beings and for manipulating and exploiting his environment (of which he is at the moment an undifferentiated part). These names and games are useful fictions, and if he is born into a culture that helps him avoid confusing the games with the realities, he will form a sort of ego net through which tentacles can be deployed for constant empathetic interaction with the world as he grows in the flow of its (and his) becoming.

But there is no such culture in the world. I doubt that there ever has been.

So instead of forming an ego *net*, our newborn human will gradually weave around himself a sort of fibrous casing, tough, perhaps translucent like the cataracts on old eyes, with few interstices for the excursion of extruded parts of himself and with little capacity for indefinite growth. It will take some years to complete this cocoon, the inside of which may contain spots of reflective surface in which he will see himself and entangle that information with the distorted information coming through from outside.

This is the lot of almost all humans born on this planet. A few manage to build efficient enough interior organization to enable them to put some energy to the task of cutting windows in this casing through which they can see things as they really are and through which they may reach to participate; a very few may knock out whole walls in order to "live outdoors," so to speak; and a small handful have apparently managed to abandon the structure of ego entirely to become wanderers under the infinite sky. According to the accounts of these people, and as nearly as we can understand or interpret, they share these points in common:

1. They suffer no thwarted desires, no fears, and appear to sustain a positive happiness.
2. They are awakened to some kind of heightened consciousness.
3. They find and proclaim the world to be unspeakably beautiful.
4. They regard time in a manner that renders each moment eternal.
5. They consider their personality as separate from and transcending their individual egos, which they regard as a fiction anyway. This gives them an identity with the universe and some kind of immortality.
6. They tout no irrational miracles, they preach no doctrine of self-denial or sin or transcendental god.
7. They claim no special divinity and regard every human as possessing the capacity to attain this height.

This degree of expansiveness is not necessary to a reasonable level of maturity, however. But if it is a proper picture of extrapolated maturity, there is apparently no good reason for not continuing as far as possible along the path. The avant-garde gives no evidence of any danger of unpleasantness in doing so.

If you have any reason to believe you are too tightly encased in the cocoon of ego, or if you feel that the external world in general is threatening and unpleasant, and after coping with it you have too little energy left over to be creative or to enjoy life, it could be that the development of an expansive attitude would make things better for you.

A step toward developing this new attitude is to reassess your vulnerability. In what way, for example, can you really be hurt by criticism? Any criticism leveled at you must either be valid or invalid. If valid, it will be worth your while to accept it and decide whether you wish to take corrective steps or not. There is no compulsion to follow any advice implied in criticism. Let us suppose you are charged with being lazy. The criticism is either true or untrue. If it is untrue and you know it to be untrue, you may be curious as to why you had given the impression, or why the person criticizing you felt obliged to accuse you of laziness. In any case, you will dismiss it as untrue and will not resent it. A clue to your certainty or uncertainty about the charge is to be found in your reaction to it. We are never angry unless something is threatened. For example, if someone were to say that you are fat, when you are in fact six feet tall and weigh 130 pounds, it will not anger you because you have no doubt in the world that the statement is groundless. It is indeed preposterous. Likewise, if someone says you have homosexual tendencies and you are certain you do not have such tendencies, your reaction will be the same, since nothing is threatened. But if you are uncertain about your gender, and are at great pains to create a positive heterosexual image to display to the world *and to yourself*, you may become quite angry with someone who has apparently seen through your façade and made bold to let you know. All angry reaction to criticism is because deep down we feel the critic may be right. If you know the criticism has no basis in fact, there is no reason for anger, and there will be none. If the criticism strikes at something you have been hiding, it can threaten you in two ways:

1. If you are consciously aware of hiding something from the outside world, the criticism threatens your ruse. You may wish to continue it for good reasons or poor reasons, but you are not fooling yourself. Or you may decide to abandon the ruse if it has been seen through.

2. If you are unconsciously hiding something from yourself, you will more deeply resent evidence that the game is up. Here you may (a) use your anger to convince yourself that the criticism and the critic are crazy or vicious or both, and bolster your self-delu-

sion with this fiction, or (b) consider the accusation and decide whether it is tolerable to accept it as a hypothesis, and from there find out if it is true. It may be that the charge is, after all, unfounded. Remember, it is not the truth or falsehood of the criticism that causes your reaction to it. It is your idea of the real state of affairs that causes the trouble by being in conflict with the image you desire to protect. If you are so detached from reality as to think deep down that you are fat when you are in fact thin, your insecurity about your weight will operate, in an accusation of being fat, *as though you were fat*. This kind of groundless insecurity shows up in people who get rich but whose need for making more and more money is rooted in the continuing feeling that they are poor. Some earlier set of experiences in life scarred them with financial insecurity, and although their brains may tell them they have more wealth than most of the people they know, the emotional warp is not straightened out with mere intellectual knowledge of their financial well-being.

In the realm of physical well-being there is one type of hypochondriac who can never for long accept evidence that he is well. Symptoms of illness, generated by some insecurity, will creep back and spoil his enjoyment of his health. Hence the wealthy man who feels poor is very sensitive to status, and the hypochondriac is extremely suggestible to comments bearing on his health. Have you ever said to a hypochondriac (not the kind who enjoys ill health, but the kind really terrified of it) that he looks pale? It can ruin his whole day, or send him to a new doctor.

Criticism may be valid or invalid, and it may or may not be advanced with hostility. A critical comment may be casual, helpful, or the result of annoyance, bursting through the restraints of caution and tact. But the only thing it can hurt is some myth you have constructed about yourself. It can never really hurt *you*.

In returning to our step to developing an expansive attitude through reassessing our vulnerability, we have found that we are essentially invulnerable. Only our self-image can be threatened or harmed or dismantled. The more the self-image coincides with what we really are, the less vulnerable it is.

The more faith we develop in this essential invulnerability, the more we are able to consider criticism from a standpoint of reason and to act on it reasonably. This is the kind of growth that allows us to move more and more outside the ego cocoon. This is the kind of growth that leads to maturity.

[3]

The "timeless" attitude enables us to invest each moment of life with a flavor of eternity, and to focus on the now. This is desirable because undue preoccupation with the past and future causes us to miss the moment, and "the moment" is what life is.

Undue preoccupation with the past and future comes from indulging in remorse about things done and dread of things to come. These things snowball because they cause us to muff opportunities that arise in the present, and this leads to more remorse and more dread of things to come.

I remember goofing a play in high school basketball, and while I brooded about it I goofed several more. I came to dread basketball. (And, I might add, basketball came to dread me.)

Kahlil Gibran speaks of "the overprudent dog, burying bones in the trackless wilderness." The Bible urges us to consider the "lilies of the field, which reap not, neither do they sow." On every hand there is advice to cut down on the amount of planning and providing and worrying about the future that we do. But still we do it, with such persistence that we often miss out on living. What future do we imagine, that we feel we can afford to miss any of the present?

Professor John R. Platt of Michigan writes in *The Step to Man*, "The only time there is, is now. The only place for you is here. You have an appointment first with the present. Where are you going so very fast? Had you forgotten that you have a rendezvous with life here, now? If you do not know how to enjoy the being and becoming of the present instant, with all its interrelated details and active potentialities waiting to be awakened, how can you ever get to a being and a becoming that you will know how to enjoy better?"

Assuming it's desirable to adopt and develop a timeless attitude, how do we go about moving toward making it a habit?

We need not, of course, abolish memory nor abandon all planning or providing for the future. It is the unnecessary, the inordinate dwelling in the past and hovering over the future that must be done away with in order to make the fullest use of the present moment. If a pill is good for you, it doesn't mean that twenty will be twenty times as good. If it is good to learn from the past and to provide for the future, it is not better to dwell in the past and to be overprovident about the future.

In setting about to prune overprudence and remorse, start with an attack on the concept of guilt. You can do this by choosing some small thing or event in which you feel you were wrong and admitting it—to yourself—and then to someone else if appropriate. It's not so difficult to say you were wrong in little things. Unless you are badly mired in the need to justify yourself at every turn, you are probably quite capable of admitting you are wrong when you are, but along with this admission should go a conscious effort to convert any contrition to constructive reparation. By that I mean if you feel bad about having wronged someone, give your attention to the *situation* and not to yourself. Correct the situation. Don't bother right away about correcting yourself. Have you through thoughtlessness or carelessness or anger, tromped on someone's toes? And do you believe you were in the wrong? Then it is appropriate (1) to feel bad about having hurt the person, (2) to correct the situation by making amends, and (3) to benefit by the experience to the extent that it will help to keep you from falling again into that particular kind of error. It is inappropriate to travel the following road (1) to feel *guilty* (2) to justify the incident in order to assuage the feeling of guilt and (3) to learn nothing from the experience. We might go so far as to say that you have a right never to feel guilty about *anything*. Guilt is almost thoroughly useless. It is worse than useless in that it is self-destructive. By attacking your total being it breeds defenses against an assault on yourself, and the defenses often take the form of justification of the specific error that caused the guilt.

Suppose you knocked down your neighbor's mailbox with your car. If deep down you are alarmed at having misjudged the positions of the car and the mailbox, and if you leap from there to the conclusion that you are stupid or inept, you are focusing your attention on your whole being and attacking yourself. If, on the other hand, you focus attention on the *incident*—the damage to the mailbox and your car and the harm done to your neighbor and his property—you will be too busy with the event—the moment at hand—to dwell on possible deep deficiencies in yourself. You will feel bad, but you need not feel guilty. After all, you didn't set about to knock over his mailbox. You can direct your energy toward making it right with him, fixing your car, and figuring out how you came to misjudge the clearance, and *then* feed back the elements of the experience into a constructive determination to avoid a repetition of that accident in particular and to improving some of your skills in general in the area of car-handling.

Again, giving attention to the moment and what is appropriate to it, guides you away from the compounding error of guilt. When you assess the damage, and go to your neighbor to help him reset his mailbox or offer to pay to have it done, you are living in the present. When you start by saying, "Why did he put his stupid mailbox in that spot in the first place?" you are going into the past. And when you follow it with a dread of the suit he may bring against you for property damage, you are living in an unnecessary future.

Guilt has the capacity to hurt us by distorting the present, forcing us to leave it for the past and future.

A little practice in this with small things will lead to habits that break up the concept of guilt and the retreat from the present. It doesn't matter whether you start by practicing "not feeling guilty" or by giving attention to the moment (the incident)—the position of the cart and the horse are unimportant here. Action in either sphere produces results in both.

The acquisition of a "timeless" attitude seems to admit of techniques made up of a conscious frontal attack rather than the oblique volitional ploys previously discussed. Once acquired, the childlike quality of timelessness in the enjoyment of life comes back into play. This is that "quality of eternity" that gives the child's (and the mature adult's) sense of time a freedom from mortality.

## [4]

What I call an "active" attitude toward life is really an attitude toward yourself as being an active person—that is, a person self-motivated, creative, spontaneous. Of course, the way to such an attitude is to "be active." As advice, this is about as useful as telling an alcoholic to "be temperate," or a terrified person to "be unafraid." They have heard it before, probably tried it before in dozens of ways, and it doesn't mean a damned thing. But they may still save themselves by some action that can be traced indirectly to advice of some kind. By what means can you become spontaneous and free and relatively unafraid of consequences of your commitments and actions? There are ways.

First, it is necessary to look carefully at the relationship between maturity or processes of maturity, and motivation. Since maturing brings on self-motivation, and self-motivation is a key to maturing, we have another of those circles. Somehow, at some point, we have to jump on the merry-go-round, which keeps whizzing by. Specific advice on accomplishing this is necessarily rather complicated.

To state that a living organism has needs that demand immediate satisfaction is an oversimplification, but it is the point from which we'll start in portraying the "active" attitude and subsequently pointing ways to it.

The newborn human does have needs, and his comfort and

happiness require and demand immediate satisfaction. Immediate satisfaction is not usually available, and it can be demonstrated that in developing methods for tolerating this fact of life, the growing infant is not merely equipping himself to function in an indifferent world, he is building techniques for deriving pleasure from a variety of sources on several different levels. It will further be seen that if it weren't for this aspect of indifference in a world that frustrates, denies, throws up obstacles, and presents at times an atmosphere of hostility, there would be no growth, no maturing, and no means of enjoying the higher forms of pleasure accessible to increasing maturity. The hostility of the world (the cold, unfeeling framework of the universe is not just something to climb on and push against) is a positive force in the realization of pleasure, working in a sort of symbiotic relationship with inner drives of the individual.

Here can be seen the very different nature of emotional maturing from physical and mental maturing. Where body growth leaps forward with an energy that diminishes as a limit is approached, and where mental ability approaches a peak of efficiency in roughly three decades, levels off, and declines, except for the compensatory effects of continued stockpiling of experience, emotional maturing appears to be an open-ended process of limitless expansion.

Although life would appear to have as a general goal the attainment of equilibrium, modern psychology has come to the view that the goal is not the reduction of tensions to the vanishing point, but rather the maintenance of tensions at some optimum level. This appears to be a primary motivation. "The living being wants total equilibrium only in the future, a future which is forever deferred."‡

From a physicist's point of view, life can be defined as an "anti-entropic" activity. Entropy is the tendency of organization to unravel, the tendency of things to go from order to chaos. This is the increase of the random element, the basis of the Second Law of Thermodynamics.

‡ Charlotte Bühler, "Maturation and Motivation."

Life appears to swim upstream in entropy. Schroedinger says that the organism keeps alive "by continually drawing from its environment negative entropy" and by avoiding maximum entropy, which is death.*

Freud believed tension to be unpleasurable except for sexual tension. Psychoanalysis might have developed differently if Freud had found parallels between the potential pleasure in many tensions and that which he acknowledged in sex.

Although not exactly parallel, there are strong similarities between this view of physical life and the psychological processes operative in human life. Looked at another way, we are constantly striving to get into total adjustment with our environment. This is impossible since the environment is not static, and when we approach adjustment the environment changes, so we must repeat the process.

Whether this ongoing lack of adjustment is to be regarded as a continual annoyance, or as a helpful external driving force, is a question of attitude. The desirability of an attitude that would see it as the latter is obvious. This is precisely the active attitude. Let's see how it is arrived at.

In addition to the pleasure of immediate gratification of wishes and immediate satisfaction of needs, there are more sophisticated pleasures at higher levels of psychological organization.

Some psychologists, among them Goldstein and Maslow, see self-actualization as the drive that carries the organism on to activity after equilibrium has been reached. And again, Bühler: "A man comes home from work, he is hungry and tired and wants to eat and to rest. After he did so and the equilibrium was re-established . . . he wants now some new activity. Why? . . . He may as well feel pleasure in satisfying his urges as in the following stage of re-acquired strength when he looks for new

* The best description I've run across of this deliberate aim of an individual to seek and maintain tensions at some optimum level is found in Fenichel's definition of homeostasis: ". . . the aim of maintaining a certain level of tension characteristic for the organism, rather than the aim of the total abolition of all tension."(Fenichel, quoted by Bühler in "Maturation and Motivation," p. 328.)

activity. The pleasure of satisfaction is one, the pleasure of being able to do things another, and pleasure is not identical with satisfaction."†

If life demands tensions and also demands easing them, it is safe to say that we seek tensions and can find pleasure in doing so. In the following cycle we see several sources of pleasure:

1. Pleasure in equilibrium momentarily attained (e.g., after eating and resting).

2. Pleasure in seeking tension (e.g., seeking new activity, or planning some new project).

3. Pleasure in acquiring tension (e.g., moving off the dead-center of equilibrium—embarking on the new undertaking).

4. Pleasure in anticipating the reduction of tensions now set up by the challenges of the new project (goal striving).

5. Pleasure in applying functions or mastering functions useful for goal attainment. (This is function pleasure, conceived by Karl Groos and other psychologists as an incentive to further practice a new function. This is part of a theory of "mastery of material" referred to in the works of Groos and Woodworth, in which attainment of a function and practicing it are considered to be basic motivating forces. This is seen most forceably in the young, in the obvious pleasure they derive from merely exercising some newly acquired skill such as walking, or throwing an object away, or riding a bicycle.)

6. Pleasure in goal attainment, which brings the individual back to equilibrium.

The difference between the self-motivated person and one who is not is that the self-motivated person recycles this process actively, whereas the merely reactive individual lets the natural continuing change in his environment provide this recycling. *The self-motivated help to create their own environmental changes that produce new tension.*

† Bühler, op. cit., pp. 330–31.

Let's take these six levels of pleasure through an individual's project to see how they apply as a concrete example.

Tom has finished a week of hard work, and on Friday evening he wants to eat and sleep. After doing so he is rested and no longer hungry, and by Saturday morning he is sensing the pleasurable state of equilibrium represented by level No. 1.

2. He drifts pleasurably toward some new activity and decides to take up spear-fishing.

3. He goes to a sporting goods store in his neighborhood and purchases diving gear and a Hawaiian sling spear, along with which he gets a free course in the rudiments of diving and diving safety. Embarking on the project has its own pleasure.

4. He sets a goal: He will spear some fish. Along with his main goal, other subsidiary goals spring up: He will master the technique of diving and spearing; he will successfully minimize danger and come back alive, etc. The anticipation of these accomplishments carries a special kind of pleasure. Tensions are produced: He must wait on the convenience of the fish—there are no fish in the practice pool, so he can't immediately gratify the wish or attain the goal of getting a catch, and there is no guarantee that fish will present themselves where he dives in the sea. So he defers the reward. But he has enough maturity to find this frustration not only tolerable but pleasurable in that it seasons the end result with an x-factor and provides a mild obstacle to work around—a sort of exercise bar at which he can flex the muscles of his determination and strengthen his drive toward his goal. In this there is also pleasure.

5. In learning how to use the equipment, he finds a great deal of pleasure. This is the "function pleasure" that turns means into tributary ends in themselves. If he goes forth and finds no fish, it will not negate the positive pleasure he will have found in learning how to dive—that will have become a goal in itself. This may be attributable in part to what Allport refers to as the "functional autonomy" of motives. Allport points to the fact that motives seem to have a life of their own in that we are

motivated to do certain things later in life, or we retain early cravings, for entirely different reasons than the original ones. "We all went to school to please mother, but we certainly do not now continue our studies for this reason." Tom may continue an interest in diving even after losing interest in spear-fishing.

6. Tom goes out Sunday with a diving party, and late in the afternoon reaches his main goal by spearing a large fish, which he can't wait to bring home. He gets home tired and hungry and will refresh himself with food and rest and thus complete the cycle, to level No. 1.

The best way to cultivate an active attitude if you feel you lack one is to meddle with fate. Create and mold some of your own tensions. Don't let others, or the world, determine in what way your environment will change, creating new challenges and tensions in you by demolishing your momentary equilibrium. Demolish it yourself, and try to do so in ways that are less capricious than if it were left to fate.

Are you certain you'll catch cold because you are prone to colds and probably due for one? Then catch it from your own action. Don't cower inside waiting for it. Go for a walk in the rain, without a raincoat. Walk through, not around puddles. At least you'll know you engineered your own cold. More likely, you will prove that you don't catch colds as easily as you thought. At any rate, you will find walking in the rain can be very enjoyable. And dress in clothes that you aren't obliged to protect. (The purpose of clothing is to protect us, yet we are continually protecting our clothing.)

Another example: "The pleasure of satisfaction is one thing, the pleasure of being able to do things is another. And pleasure is not identical with satisfaction." The phrase "getting there is half the fun" shows this. If you have a job to do, the goal is completion of the job. But pleasure can be found in each operation moving you toward the goal. Take apart any task you undertake and open yourself to the possibility that each fragment of it can be enjoyable. Don't focus all the time on the ultimate goal. You'll miss good things whizzing by. And you won't be able to divide and conquer because the ultimate goal may be overwhelmingly large, and the small steps that could be pleasurable will seem so puny that they will be flavored with futility.

Always mix business and pleasure. It has been said, "If you don't find pleasure in your work, you won't find pleasure."

The Puritan notion that all virtuous actions are unpleasurable and that anything enjoyable is to be regarded with suspicion gave us the admonition not to mix business with pleasure. The implicit assumption that "business" had to be devoid of pleasure is typical. The most creative people I know, and some of the happiest, are those who constantly mix business with pleasure.

I struggled with the business of broadcasting for at least a dozen years in dead seriousness. I made neither a name nor any money in it until I started having fun with it. I can't say that the change in attitude was the result, in this instance, of any conscious effort on my part, at least not in the way of a plan. It came, rather, from seeing broadcasting as a man-killing business that had driven several colleagues to drink and death and realizing (1) I wanted to avoid that, and (2) I was free to bail out of it and do something else. Then having decided to quit, I found that I didn't have to take it so seriously and began to have fun with it. I have never since decided *not* to quit, but have left it open, as it should be always with any trade or profession.

This is a kind of "You can't fire me, I quit" attitude, which somehow has the effect of diminishing the punishments fate deals out. Again, as advice it seems a bit silly, and as any kind of therapy, in the orthodox sense, it makes no claim to substitute for or improve on psychiatric techniques. I am not addressing it to patients or candidates for psychotherapy. If you are ill, you should consider and seek professional help. If, however, you know you are able to function, but are not realizing your full potential; if you believe you could be a little freer of cultural restrictions and cloying obligations than you are; if you think you are more at the mercy of fate than you'd like to be; and above all, if you recall that the world of your childhood was a little more interesting than the one you are moving in now, you represent a high percentage of us all, and this is directed to you.

[5]

Developing a generic attitude must deal with the tenuous and mysterious bridge between intellectual understanding and emotional knowing. And it must also show how very limited are ascetic gestures and self-denial. For very limited objectives, self-denial can be called into play with some effectiveness, but it is treacherous and not of value for long-range goals, as will be shown presently.

Many minds are attracted to the idea of a "unifying philosophy of life" and recruit their intellectual apparatus in the construction of a system purporting to model the universe. Different philosophies may represent what constitutes aesthetic appeal to the adherent, who may feel he has extracted a set of truths that go to make up his model, where in reality he has chosen his material according to what is emotionally tolerable to him. It's possible that no picture of the universe intellectually graspable by humans is anywhere near the reality of the universe, if indeed any such "reality" in the sense of an ultimate knowable external truth exists.

But a certain type of enlightenment seems to have been attained by a few humans, who although they arrived at it independently and often from different starting points, share agreement on certain aspects of it.

It is, they agree, not scientifically or intellectually analyzable. It is not vulnerable to attack by rational means. It is more related to modes of action than to concepts. It is neither a state of being nor a goal-directed evolution, but rather an eternal becoming, both the totality and each minute differentiation of which are miraculous. Any portion of it, when isolated, is seen to be a fiction or illusion, including human individuals.

Toward the end of the past century science began to circumscribe itself. It got a glimpse of its limitations in acknowledging that it will never describe what something *is*, only what it *does*. The work of Maxwell, Lorentz, Einstein, and Planck forced matter virtually to evaporate: atomic particles, once viewed as tiny bits of hard substance with electric charges, were found to be merely the electric charges having a location in space. They became nothing more than their "influences" on the surrounding environment. The equivalence of mass and energy showed mass-energy to be a force in the cosmos. But almost simultaneously both the force and the space it was imagined to be contained in crumbled. The "force" was reduced to a geometric component in a multidimensional continuum of which space was three dimensions (any three) and time one (any one), the whole thing bent in still another dimension. So space and time became interchangeable. Heisenberg, in trying to reconcile wave and particle theories of matter, glimpsed an almost limitless number of dimensions and then came to see that the dimensional concept was a device for dealing rationally with material phenomena. Eddington felt toward the end of his life that concepts of space, time, matter, and energy were more a reflection of our method of thinking than of any truth about the physical world. Einstein, having abolished the ether, abolished space, the very home of these "forces" or "influences" to which he had already reduced matter, and thereby translated the geometric aspects of mass-energy to pure mathematics (which is pure thought), rendering the universe a gigantic thought rather than a substantial machine.

Scientist E. R. Laithwaite, in a private communication to the author, indicated his belief that the concept of the atomic structure of matter is probably false, but useful for dealing with matter.

Science grew up when it came face to face with its limitations. It is still useful, as is Euclidean geometry (which is now known to be valid only in a universe containing no matter whatever), but science will not lead us to the kind of insights we seek.

Logic and the mathematics of symbolic logic have begun turning up cracks in their own structure. It had long been suspected that the axioms, once thought self-evident, on which systems of logic rested, might be questionable, but recently mathematicians have explored gaping holes in the edifice of logic itself. Logic, if it does not dismantle itself, may yet limit itself in the way science has done.

Before science and logic began to grow up in this way— before modern science was born—sages of the type characterized by the generic outlook bypassed science and intellectual speculation altogether in favor of direct emotional or spiritual contact with the world. It was not so much that they were puzzled about scientific things and gave up, as that they regarded science from the outset as not pertinent to the truths they felt or sought or preached. It was as though we looked to baseball as a way of life. There are things to be known about baseball, and self-consistent rules and laws, and it can be interesting, but it is not "real" even to the players.

What the sages were onto is more of the nature of revealed truth than factual truth. Plato said, "The fact is mortal, the idea immortal." We all know that today's fact may be tomorrow's fallacy, while revealed truths are unassailable.

As an example of a revealed or inner truth, suppose I were to claim that more people in the United States enjoyed horseback riding than swimming. And suppose you claim the reverse. One of us is right, and the other is wrong. A little research can resolve the issue. One of us will be surprised, perhaps, to find he was wrong. What he thought was a truth is vulnerable to outside evidence. But now suppose we got into the following argument: You say *you prefer* swimming to horseback riding. And I say you prefer horseback riding to swimming. You know that you are right and I am wrong. And you know that your knowledge is not vulnerable. You know that no amount of research on my part, in all the libraries of the world, no interviews I might conduct with your friends or yourself, no theories I might concoct would topple or even endanger the truth of your viewpoint. Revealed truth is of this interior kind. If an enlightened person really identifies with the universe (becomes one with it as it becomes one with him), then all his truths about it are of this "interior" kind. Now we can see why he wastes no time worrying about any advance of science or any activity of intellect being able to threaten what he knows. What he knows is not a matter of intellect, and not subject to what may be fashionable for the moment.

Second, his truths are more related to modes of action than to concepts. Consider again Bertrand Russell's sausage machines. Studying the interior mechanism is not a profitable thing for a sausage machine to do. Making sausages is. Truth is here identical with fulfillment rather than fact. The great religions of the world speak more of paths and ways than of truths. Paths and ways are to be trod, not studied on maps.

Although tales of irrational miracles crept into the biographies of the world's really great, they themselves seem to have had little use for trickery of this sort. They seem rather to have sensed the miraculous quality of life itself. "My miracle is that when I am hungry I eat and when I am thirsty I drink," said the Zen Buddhist monk Bankei. And a respected scientist says, ". . . God is not some kind of watchmaker as the old apologists mechanically wished us to suppose. They were as deceived as all the other mechanists, from not looking closely enough at the flowers of the field. The factory that makes the parts of a flower is inside, and is not a factory but a development. God is more like a chromosome or a thought, than a watchmaker. The creative principle of the universe and its organization and intelligence is not an external principle but an internal one. All the past that we can ever know is contained in the world at this instant. All the evolving potentiation of the future are contained in the world at this instant. And men are the carriers of this active potentiality as much as any. The creative principle is inside of you and me. A single protein molecule or a single fingerprint, a single syllable on the radio or a single idea of yours, implies the whole historical reach of stellar and organic evolution. It is enough to make you tingle all the time."‡

This is not mysticism, at least not of the transcendental type.

‡ John R. Platt, *The Step of Man*, p. 183.

Immanent mystics, if they should be called mystics at all, are not in conflict with science, but rather they do not give it much importance as far as truth is concerned. Their truths do not call for anything contrary to intellect or science but appear to be beyond them.

Gordon Allport says, "Some men . . . are 'immanent mystics,' that is, they find their religious experience in the affirmation of life and in active participation therein. The transcendental mystic, on the other hand, seeks to unite himself with a higher reality by withdrawing from life; he is the ascetic, and . . . finds the experience of unity through self-denial and meditation."

Without presuming to judge these types of "mystics," one could make a case for the superior maturity of the immanent over the transcendental, in that withdrawal from the world and one's fellow men is less empathetic, less "unified." Whereas St. Simeon Stylites and Bodhidharma dropped out completely to meditate, Jesus Christ and Gautama Buddha were no recluses—they remained active and in public.

Is it necessary to become in any sense a mystic to achieve a degree of maturity? Is it necessary to abandon speculation about science and all intellectual pursuits in order to attain the kind of truth that is unassailable? Is it necessary to give up earthly pleasures in order to find greater ones, whatever they are?

Here is a case of the positioning of cart and horse. Enlightened men did not gain enlightenment by giving up all these things so important to less mature men. It was the other way around: They gave up the pleasures we deem important *because they had become enlightened.* One of them, Buddha, made it quite clear through his own futile experience that asceticism—self-denial—did nothing to enlighten him. He proclaimed it to be as empty as hedonism—indulging sensual pleasure—as a means to awakening.

If the rich young man had followed Jesus' advice to sell all he had and give to the poor, it would probably have done nothing for him (although it would have done something for a few of the poor). What he was urged to do was to care so intensely about the poor and all mankind that his wealth would have been as nothing to him. In this circumstance he would have given it willingly. There would have been no sacrifice involved. In this kind of salvation nothing is forced. Who can hinder you from loving, from caring?

You did not give up your tricycle in order to grow up. You gave up your tricycle *because you had grown up*. A little girl doesn't abandon her dolls in order to become a mother. She has, as a mother, no need of dolls.

Exhortations to behave in a manner of great wisdom are usually vain. Self-denial on a sudden and grand scale is usually only a result (or a cause) of pride of a particularly pernicious sort. If, a step at a time, we unfold into wisdom and maturity, we may relinquish earlier pleasures, not cutting them away surgically, but watching them slough off.

What I seem to be saying is that we cannot move toward maturing by any means accessible to our volition. This is true only if we demand direct results by direct action. But there is a connection between desire to mature and action resulting from that desire, and between the action itself and maturing. The connection is not direct. If you stand at the bars of your cage and see freedom on the other side, and you cannot attain it by assailing the bars, the cage door may yet be open behind you. Attaining freedom may require turning away from it momentarily.

There is no frontal attack on a generic outlook or "enlightenment" or maturing. If you aspire to build a penthouse, start with the foundation of a building on which it will be perched. Each step of the way is possible for each of us.

The totality itself is not immediately attractive to all of us. To many, it seems too difficult, too godlike, too cold and lonely, too forbidding. We don't want to change *that* much.

When my mother was a little girl she was invited to taste watermelon. She had decided she wouldn't like it, and she declined. Her older sister urged her to try it, because since she had never tasted it she couldn't know that she didn't like it, and she might find she *did* like it. "That's what I'm afraid of," said my mother, "if I tasted it and liked it, I'd eat it, and I hate it." One of the sources of anger in the defense of one's prejudices is a deep-down fear that one may *lose* one's prejudices.

# CHAPTER VIII

## *Mental Judo*

[1]

If the intellect is adequate to encompass higher kinds of wisdom,
is there any kind of connection between the two that makes intellect useful in the *pursuit* of wisdom? The rational mind is a
tool, much as muscles and senses are tools. Hands and eyes cannot
give knowledge by any direct means, but hands can hold a book
and turn the pages, and eyes can transmit images of letters and
words through the optic nerve into the brain. Likewise intellectual
speculation, even if unable to force interior truths, or condition
emotional set, can help create a milieu—a culture—in which insight may be encouraged to breed.

There is a parallel in the so-called "music appreciation" courses
given in schools. I have never found the slightest direct connection
between the history of music, or the biographies of composers or
even the analyses of scores, and the aesthetic content of the music
—which is what it's all about. But a course that deals with these
external things and that plays and dissects music creates some interest, sets a mood, and exposes the student to the material. From
this he may well develop a real appreciation, even though quite
indirectly. One thing is certain: No music was ever appreciated

that was never heard (for the purists "heard" is here defined as including "read from a score and 'heard' in the mind").

In applying volition to techniques of maturing, or in applying it to the delicate task of setting up a nest or house into which natural processes of maturing hopefully will be lured, we haven't turned enough attention to utilization of weaknesses as well as strengths. Earlier, we set a value on knowing your limitations—both as a member of the human race and as an individual who may have some special limitations. Pending the correction of these deficiencies (or adjustment to them if they are unchangeable), they can be put to use. An example: If you are shy in group gatherings, you can try to force yourself to overcome your shyness, or you can sit among the group worrying about your inability to overcome shyness, or you can put it to use in a way that will remove it as a target and allow it to dismantle itself. Shyness takes the conscious form of fear that your utterances will be received poorly—either laughed at, or scorned, or ignored. The feeling is, "I'd rather not contribute at all than be misunderstood or derided." Here is a good problem to turn your back on. This is an example of the third type of oblique volition: Do nothing about it. Brooding about it won't do, because brooding about it is *doing* something about it instead of ignoring it. Obviously you can't sit there and concentrate on not brooding about it, so how do you do nothing about it? Again, remember the way the sentence was restressed to make it possible: "Do nothing about *it*." If you are shy and this is the problem you wish to tackle, turn your back on it and use it to accomplish something else.

A person who talks a great deal when he's in a group has less opportunity to listen than one who talks little. If you tend not to talk at all, this gives you maximum opportunity to listen. Forget about being shy. Now you are no longer silent for the negative reason of being afraid to contribute, but for the positive reason of desiring to listen as carefully as possible to everything that is said. Shyness is now no longer a factor. Your mind is off that quality of yours. Your mind is off the problem. The more you become absorbed in other people's contributions, the more you think about the subject matter and the less about yourself. But two things happen: By "letting go" of the problem, it breaks a deadlock of self-consciousness; and by listening carefully to the contributions of others, knowledge is gained that reduces the likelihood that anything you might say would be inappropriate and laughed at (this is the fear at the base of the shyness). The topics of conversation need not be profound or even important. Much is learned about people from their small talk. After a bit you may tend to forget you are shy and your first breakthrough may be spontaneous laughter at something funny, or vocal agreement or disagreement at something said, or a surprisingly effortless answer to a question put to you.

In this address to the problem you have applied a kind of mental judo. You have forced the problem to cooperate in leverage against itself much as a judo expert directs his opponent's own strength against himself.

An example of the second type of oblique volition applied to a problem involving weakness is seen in the case of a woman unable to pass a dish of candy or nuts without eating them. She is overweight. All frontal attacks on the problem have proved valueless. She rationalizes that the candy-and-nut dishes in her home are for reasons of hospitality—that guests may want them. Finally, she realizes that she will never force herself to develop the willpower to pass by a nut-laden bowl or candy-filled dish (and she may suspect her real reason for having them around), so she removes the temptation from her surroundings by not having them in her house. The control of temptation is often more important than the development of strength against it.

So three ways to deal with weaknesses fairly acknowledged to be in oneself are: (1) If appropriate, forget them. If you have a trick knee or a back that goes out when you lift heavy things, and you've really put your best efforts into bringing it up to full strength and have finally concluded it will never be even up to average, live with it. It can be worked around. (2) If the weakness is one of purpose or will, manipulate those elements of environment that surround it. Give it a chance to become a strength by protecting it from being overwhelmed. (If you want to stop drinking before lunch and ruining your afternoon, don't continue futilely to "not order a drink" while others are doing so. Instead, have lunch at a restaurant that has no liquor license.) (3) If the weakness is made worse by focusing on it, then use the "mental judo" on it by ignoring it while using some property of it to heighten attention to a related (or unrelated) project.

[2]

Again, I'd like to stress the deeply different nature of emotional maturing, as I've chosen to describe it, from physical and mental maturing. Analogies among the three are awkward. They are the same in that they all move toward increase of organization; they all have some spontaneous or inner vitality; they all require nutrients of some sort; they all admit some degree of purposeful manipulation—i.e., that respond to volition, at least indirectly; and they are all vulnerable to arrest. But while physical and mental maturation slack off as they approach limits, emotional maturity apparently does not; while physical maturing translates its drive at that limit to sexual reproduction and goes on in new individuals, mental maturing does not have this characteristic. (Emotional maturing does appear to have it in a way explored below.) And whereas both physical and mental maturity describe natural trajectories of increase-peak-decline, emotional maturity can be arrested or forced into decline only by factors that operate obstructively against a scalar or possibly exponential increase of limitless potential.

Emotional maturity seems less a state than a system, a process analogous to fire, which is a flow system, capable of expanding without limit in the presence of combustibles and oxygen. The emotional aspects of "becoming" (which would indicate that it is preferable to speak not of "emotional maturity" but rather "emotional maturing") seems to transcend individuality, but not in the discrete way physical maturing does (that is, by instituting the device of carrying on through physical reproduction) at the time that size limit is approached. Emotional maturing creates, through its components of empathy and sympathy, a milieu that encourages the emotional maturing *of other individuals*. This could be regarded as a kind of reproduction. In other words, a mature individual exerts on others a force not merely helpful or kindly, but conducive to maturing. Whereas merely adequate parents, for example, may be seen to feed and instruct and protect their children, dutifully and even lovingly, parents who have themselves matured add to these practices a constant salute to the independence and unique humanness of each child, encouraging emotional growth and diminishing dependency.

Suppose we find ourselves stronger than someone else, so much stronger that his weakness means a very real need on his part, that he is being crushed by the burdens of his life. We, having strength to spare, may want to shoulder some of his burden. We are moved to help him. This is commendable, but also a little smug. For one thing, it helps to assure us of our superiority. Much charity, many good deeds are tainted with this.

Now, suppose we have it in our power to do a much greater thing for him, to give him a gift of infinitely more value. Let us suppose that we can give him the strength he lacks, so that he can lift his own burden and, like us, shoulder the burdens of still others. Suppose we have it in our power to make him our equal. Here is a much better gift, devoid of smugness and selfishness.

This is the aim of what is called the mental health movement. In its ultimate goal it means not merely caring for those who have collapsed under emotional strain, not merely the custodial and analgesic aspects of asylum, but the restoring of salvageable minds and above all the preventive measures and the guidance to maturity that constitute the greatest gift, the highest service of man to man.

The idea of mental and emotional health is probably older than civilization. There were people in the most ancient times whose thinking was impaired and who were silly or dangerous to themselves and others. Though only certain forms of aberrant behavior were recognized, and though these were most often imagined to be caused by demons, they were at least recognized as extraordinary.

The word "sane" derives from a classic root meaning, simply, health. "Insane" means "unhealthy"—nothing more. "Insane" is now discarded by that mechanism of politeness that changes euphemisms regularly, like bandages. However euphemistic other outmoded words for describing emotional disorder—madness, lunacy, mania, derangement, not to mention amentia and phrenitis—they all have short tenure. Painful and unpleasant things suffer frequent shifts of name.

But the ancients, even though able to spot only symptoms of irrationality in a person and prone to describe dangerous and emotionally immature people as merely wicked, did sense it as a health problem; and the words "sane" and "insane," meaning healthy and unhealthy, are quite suitable to a description of the human condition.

In the twelfth century, the great physician Maimonides wrote to the Sultan Saladin's son: "My lord . . . should know that emotional experiences cause marked changes in the body that are clear and visible. . . ."

In the first of the Upanishads, those writings of the pre-Sanskritic culture that culminated in Buddhism, is written a line that almost summarizes Carl Jung's psychology: "There are two selves, the apparent self and the real self. Of these it is the real self . . . alone [that] must be felt as truly existing. . . . The mortal in whose heart the knots of ignorance are untied becomes immortal." Here, centuries before the Christian Era, is an almost orthodox Freudian admonition to face up to the truth about one's self.

And yet, only in recent years have the concept, the diagnostic techniques, and the range of treatments broadened to include some understanding of incipient stages of mental illness, and a glimpse of hope for both individual and social maturity.

[3]

We are still prone to view the problem simplistically: to see in terms of people who are sick or well against the background of a social order assumed to be healthy.

But there is an increasing awareness that a society, too, can be ill. How else can we explain prolonged social injustice, environmental degradation, protracted wars not wanted by any of the masses of people involved, high incidences of emotional breakdown, alcoholism, suicide, and delinquency? We saw a whole culture captured in the twentieth century by an incredibly vicious ideology and stabilized long enough to blunt a national conscience for a generation, to elevate the emotionally stunted and sadistic to positions of power, and to give official sanction to the extermination of thirteen million humans, six million of whom were of one religion. And Willy Brandt, when he was mayor of Berlin, told me in a television interview, "There is a Nazi potential in every country."

We had a guest once on NBC's "Today" program who was an expert on ants. Among the many fascinating things he showed and told about these little creatures was that no individual ant ever starves. Unless the whole community dies for lack of food, it can't happen. They feed each other. Later, a staff member asked me if I thought ants might be superior to us. It depends on what we are measuring, I suppose. In physical size of the individual, we are larger than any ant—and thus superior. In intellect, the individual human is vastly superior to the individual ant (or any community of ants).

But still as a community we either display a weakness or a confusion of goals. There are nearly four billion humans on the earth. One billion eats well and wastes food; at least two billion go to bed hungry much of the time. And many starve. The food is at hand—more than enough—and the distribution of it is well within our technical capability. But we don't distribute it. And much mischief is brewed by such appalling callousness. It could not happen in an ant colony. In this one way we are inferior to the ant.

Whatever contribution social sickness makes to the over-all problem, we still have sick individuals, we still have distressed loved ones, we still have wounded fellows, and we must deal with them now, whatever the pace or state of social progress.

As more is found out about individual emotional health, more will be accomplished not only in healing those who have broken, not only in supporting those who are under intolerable stress, not only in preventing runaway tension in those who might become victims, but in providing environments in which corrective action will become less and less necessary.

What we have come to call the mental health movement can help to lay a foundation for environments that will allow a great majority in the human community to mature fully. As the human community at large matures, there should be less breakdown, there should be a diminishing of hysterical and psychosomatic disorders (and concomitantly a chance for the control and elimination of the major threats to survival: environmental pollution, starvation, and war). Half of all hospital beds are now occupied by the emotionally ill. This fraction could be reduced substantially.

Do we give to the needy? Do we believe "the poor we will always have with us?" An emotionally healthy community might emulate the ants in the distribution of food.

In an emotionally mature community we would not have great numbers of people warped into a need to fail. We would eliminate the prejudice and cruelty and despair that create ghettos and widespread poverty and drug addiction; and we would provide an early atmosphere of motivation and incentive for the capable, healing for the damaged, and understanding for those in need of rehabilitation.

Let us suppose, again, that the whole human community is brought to such a degree of maturity and emotional health that it no longer needs to transform knowledge into political power, that it can recruit leadership from the wise and compassionate rather than from the ranks of the ambitious and power-hungry, that it does finally and fully end wars. It is often observed that if the human resources now poured into armaments were to be lavished on medical research, goals of cure and prevention, even for dreaded physical diseases, would be attained much more quickly.

Less than two hundred years ago, the political experiment that represented the American Dream was considered totally unrealistic by many sober observers. Less than a hundred years ago, automotive power, the electric light, and the telephone would have been too "far out" to consider as anything but science fiction. Less than fifty years ago, psychiatric techniques now proved capable of saving countless minds didn't exist, and twenty-five years ago, tranquilizers, chemotherapy, molecular biology, and space travel were yet to come. It is not too utopian to imagine that the future—the near future—holds the potential for an end to widespread emotional illness and, as a consequence, an end to much tragedy and waste of human resources.

Imagine a crowd of people in a large, dark room. As they move about, they cut and bruise themselves on the sharp edges of the furniture. Because of this painful situation, a number of helping groups come into being: one group folds bandages for those who cut themselves on the furniture, another gropes about and rounds off sharp edges with files, and so forth. But one group addresses the problem by bringing light into the room, and in so doing it solves the problems of all the other groups.

This is the nature of any effort to enhance maturity, statistically or individually.

It is certainly true that we have come a long way from Bedlam. We have reduced, to some extent, the stigma of emotional disorder. We have educated the press to a somewhat more enlightened view of the problem (although we have not been able to keep it from sensationalizing news-making actions of what it calls "former mental patients"). We have, through tranquilizers, ended forever the hellish sounds on the old "violent wards." We have new emphasis on outpatient clinics and halfway houses. We have seen hospital stays shortened. We have awakened belatedly to the critical needs of the mentally ill child. The old, big, custodial mental hospital may be on its way to extinction. We are beginning to rehabilitate those who recover. We are getting away from the public idea that "anyone who goes to see a psychiatrist ought to have his head examined." The emotional health of a citizenry is a matter of total public concern and commitment.

[4]

One of the ways intellect can serve the maturing process is in distinguishing between useful and useless reactions, both physical and emotional. The intellect does this automatically. If its findings are palatable to the emotions—congruent with emotional needs—the data occupy consciousness, and action taken will be based on them.

A physical example can be found in pain; pain is a special interpretation of stimuli acting on sensory nerves. If you back into a hot stove, the pain is quite useful in getting you away from it. Without the stimulus (and the interpretation of it as painful), you might remain unaware of the situation until you smelled burned flesh. The intractable pain of terminal cancer, however, is quite useless. A victim knows, long since, what its message is. He may have done everything in his power, physically and mentally, to correct the situation, and peace would be preferable to the continual loud reminder of crisis. Useless pain is a fire bell that keeps on ringing after all the firefighters have arrived at the scene. It would be desirable to turn it off.

In the realm of emotions, there is also useless pain; unnecessary anxiety, grief, guilt, fear, and anger, which may have had a function at some early stage of a crisis, persist, and in persisting, constitute a drain of energy and an obstruction to remedy.

Intellect can be useful in converting pain from a tyrant to a sentinel. As the science of medicine has developed analgesics and anesthetics, psychiatry and chemotherapy are providing techniques and chemicals to reduce or suppress disturbances in the psyche that produce unnecessary and overstated emotional reactions.

What can the individual do about developing the ability to discriminate between useful and useless pain and then utilizing the knowledge?

He can develop a basis for judging intellectually (1) what areas warrant making the effort to separate the useful and the useless, (2) a picture of what constitutes long-range good for him and how it is served by acknowledging or disregarding pain, and (3) the best techniques for dealing with pain on a level of interpretation. Let's take these point by point.

1. Not all areas of pain need be put into the jurisdiction of the intellect. For example, valuable time would be lost if a reflex action were replaced by an intelligent action.

To go back to our hot stove. It is preferable to bound away from it reflexively, without thinking, rather than to have so disciplined the interpretation of stimuli that one thinks and reacts as follows: "There is evidence of intense heat on my backside. This could be damaging to tissue. I perceive now, in turning my head around and seeing a stove, that I have come in contact with it. I'd better move away."

In this sense the initial pain and the reflex it triggers are quite useful. There will be residual pain if a burn occurs, and in early life this gentle reminder may help to set patterns of caution that will keep us out of trouble. But a grown person has no real use of this aftermath, and it would be good if such pain could be intellectually turned off, or emotionally reinterpreted as stimulus but not pain.

In maturing into a way of life, we more or less decide that there are small, useless aftermaths to reflexes, emotionally as well as physically, and we may choose not to waste time trying to change them.

Short-term annoyances and anxieties following some triggering emotional response, if they mar an hour or dampen a day, need not be cause for psychiatric attention or a massive effort to eradicate. If you were frightened by a narrow escape on the highway, this fear may be useful to sharpen your attention and produce enough extra adrenalin to increase alertness for a while. On the other hand, ongoing worry is not useful, once you've dealt with the emergency.

2. Maturing involves, as noted earlier, the formation of some sort of life pattern, a flexible ideal of what kind of person you want to become. Within this picture it is desirable to decide what stimuli should be interpreted as pain and what should not. The pattern of those decisions changes throughout life.

Pain is stimulus given as interpretation involving a component of alarm. This can be demonstrated by showing the evolution of interpretation of given sets of stimuli. One of the great bases of fear is the unknown. An unfamiliar stimulus is threatening and fearful. The fear is the ingredient that determines that the stimulus should be regarded as pain.

Hence an infant regards a bowel movement as painful. The same set of stimuli, when familiar, become tolerable because they are no longer fearful and hence no longer judged to be painful. Still later in life, satisfaction can be derived from these stimuli. And an older person, conditioned to the knowledge that failure of this necessary process of elimination *is* fearful, derives positive pleasure from a bowel movement. Clearly, whether sensory stimuli are painful or pleasurable depends on how they are interpreted.

Generally, those stimuli that accompany tissue damage are interpreted as painful throughout life, but even this kind can be reinterpreted by an altered outlook. Under great stress and excitement, in the heat of battle or the dictates of pride or fashion, or with great willpower, pain can be overridden and ignored—in some cases it is reported as not having been "painful" at the time. Women can undergo the most exquisite torture to appear in public in fashionable guise; in the excitement of physical emergencies such as an accident, people have been unaware of injuries. A Tarquin king is reported to have so regretted signing a certain document that he burned off his right hand in the flame of a brazier without changing his facial expression.

3. Intelligence can be applied to much of this interpretive process only indirectly, through the manipulation of emotional attitudes. It is not easy. But I believe it is possible.

In the same way that a stimulus can be reinterpreted from painful (to the infant), to tolerable (young child), to satisfying (grown person), to pleasurable (older person), a disturbing emotion can be examined, tolerated, and transformed into something positive. Feelings are not exorcised or banished; what melts away is the "disturbing" element when the feeling is reinterpreted.

A character in Thomas Mann's *Magic Mountain* speaks of "getting used to not getting used to" a certain condition. This process transforms the condition into something less formidable.

I suspect that the normal physical decline of the body from the midtwenties on, if thrust suddenly on the very young, would be interpreted as intensely painful. What we do is "get used to" this process, and in adopting a resignation to tolerate whatever rate of change we find going on, we "get used to not getting used to" any given state. We accommodate (emotionally) the fact (and the rate) of change.

Thus a healthy emotional attitude draws its stability from a process of adapting to the decline of the physical organism it has as host. Looked at from inside, the emotional center of life *displays* its stability by adapting to the decline of the physical organism to which *it* is host. In cases of highly mature insight, in which the emotional center transcends individuality, it appears to regard the body as being incidental and less real than its true self, somewhat in the manner that Plato's cave wall shadows are not as real as whatever was supposed to be causing them.

An astonishing characteristic of the process of emotional maturing shows it to be relatively independent of physical and mental aging. Unless it is imprisoned and choked by emotional scars and callouses developed and kept intact throughout much of early life, the vitality of the maturing drive shows through even severe physical handicaps and rides above declining physical and mental powers. Examples of vital aging can be cited in such men as Bertrand Russell, G. B. Shaw, Edward Steichen, and Konrad

Adenauer; and even through severe sensory deprivation such as suffered by Helen Keller, the vital drive, like a liquid finding fissures for outlet, comes through in beauty.

It would seem that mental deterioration would render any emotional progress impossible. Brain damage from physical or chemical causes does make it difficult for a person to maintain either his capacity to deal with the outside world or the stability of his internal organization. It is the same with psychopathology. This should put a halt to further growth of any kind. But even here there are exceptions. A victim of cerebral palsy has led a dedicated life of creative research. (Cerebral palsy was, for a long time, considered a form of insanity.) There are cases of neuroses, severe enough to impair or eclipse rational functioning, through which nevertheless some form of personality integrity such as creative artistry shone. Composer Gustav Mahler, an early patient of Freud, penned in the margin of sketches for his Tenth Symphony phrases that some commentators have taken as indications of insanity. And yet this symphony is considered by many to be his greatest.

Why then are some old people (and some not so old) seen to decay emotionally along with the decay of the body? Some human psyches, in fact, crystallize or deteriorate ahead of the body.

Is the intuitive aspect of life, the spirit or vital drive, the potential to mature—are these to be considered some sort of parcel dealt out to each individual at birth, like an electric battery? Are some individuals greater than others in these respects because they were endowed with more powerful batteries at the outset, or because they made more efficient use of the current, wasting less of it in short-circuits and unnecessary drains?

Or is this drive nonindividual? Is it a vast store from which all may draw? And do individuals vary then in their capacity to draw from "house current" rather than in their intrinsic individual power? When the will to go on maturing or even the will to live are seen to shrivel or collapse in an individual, is this the drying up of some resource, or does it mean that the access to a universal resource has been overwhelmed by some opposing or obstructing agency, such as a need for self-punishment or Freud's "death instinct"?

These are philosophical questions. Perhaps they are religious questions. I do not know the answers. If we incline toward one view over the other, it may be more a reflection of need or aesthetic appeal than of what is "true." But it would appear to be at least more useful to work with the latter or oceanic view—that individuals are not isolated entities but rather have access to some common store of vitality ultimately nonindividual. The price of this is ego. But then ego is expendable—it appears to be more a cause of trouble than an asset. It has been said that "no one can afford to support an ego—his own or someone else's."

Truth often seems to be more a matter of what works than what may fit into an intellectual concept.

If you are marooned on an island off the shipping lanes, it may be more useful to believe that a ship will come by and to keep your signal fire ready and your morale high than to know the "truth" of whether a ship will ever appear. Once again, the deepest truth may have its roots in action rather than fact.

David Riesman, in a memorandum to the Kansas City Study of Middle Age and Aging (January 1953), and again in his book *The Lonely Crowd*, separates aging people into three kinds: autonomous, adjusted, and anomic. Some individuals have access to what he calls "psychological sources of self-renewal." "Aging brings for them accretions of wisdom with no loss of spontaneity and ability to enjoy life, and they are relatively independent of the culture's strictures and penalties imposed on the aged. Other individuals, possibly the majority, bear within them no such resources but are the beneficiaries of a cultural preservative (derived from work, power, position, etc.) which sustains them although only so long as the cultural conditions remain stable and protective. A third group, protected neither from within nor from without, simply decay."

The presumption of advising the aged (particularly from one

neither aged nor expert in geriatrics) is at best amusing. Advice to peer groups and younger people is presumption enough.

I have no advice, no formulas or symbolic amulets to ward off catabolisms and the eventual triumph of entropy over our physical machinery. But what follows may be flavored by and utilized as advice.

Looked at from the perspective of what we like to call reality (a peculiar and arbitrary slicing of the universe into space and time, and contact with elements through a handful of limited sense organs), we were each of us consigned to death at the moment of conception, and the best we can get out of our brief and precarious existence is peace through some sort of resignation or some hope of a mythical immortality earned by good behavior.

There is another way of looking at our situation, however—a way at least equally valid and, I believe, more useful. Let's start by acknowledging our limitations. Is it possible that our idea of "reality"—our picture of the universe (and our lives as parts of it) is sour or harsh or limited because our apparatus for perceiving it is inadequate? Our capacity is limited. (The ocean, to a five-gallon bucket, is five gallons.) If we take a snapshot with a camera having a small, dirty, distorted lens, we will get a dim, hazy, distorted picture. To call this reality is to presume that our camera was perfect. It is rationally sound and scientifically accurate to acknowledge that our ideas of size and power are limited to the order of magnitude in which we exist and function; that we see as visible light a very thin slice of the electromagnetic spectrum; that our concepts of density, temperature, time, and distance are extremely circumscribed. With such partial grasp, such limited understanding, such distorted, dim, and fragmentary glimpses as we have of everything, can we not safely assume that the universe is at least different and more than we perceive it to be?

On that assumption, is it not equally plausible that we ourselves, as parts of that universe, are different and more than we perceive ourselves to be? Are not our limitations more in perception and understanding than in being? Without demanding to understand all, is there not comfort in Eddington's words when he spoke of not only the humility that comes with contemplating the immensity of the universe, but the pride to which we are entitled, by saying, "we are citizens of no mean city"?

Consider the possibility and try to act on it without first proving it, that it is never too late or too early to strive for and achieve the kind of wisdom we have seen operative in a few people, which diminishes pain, increases both zest and peace, and in the end, in its own special way, defeats death.

Consider the possibility and try to act on it without first proving it, that whatever discomfort comes with such action, it will be less than anticipated, and in the long run deemed a small price for the gains made.

Consider the possibility and try to act on it without first proving it, that this is not a matter of special grace given to special people; that no matter what handicaps you may have, no matter how many years have been wasted, no matter how late you start, it is in your power to get up and walk out of your prison.

Consider the possibility and try to act on it without first proving it, that such an achievement is not only possible but inevitable unless you take action opposing it by saying "nonsense" or "it can't be done" or "I'd try it but I'm afraid it would be too uncomfortable [or ridiculous or useless]."

There are conditions where the counterfeiting of a feeling may bring on an atmosphere that allows the real feeling to flower. Analogous to the music appreciation course which, although it can't force an aesthetic appreciation of music, does contribute obliquely to the development of appreciation by providing an environment that not only includes music but a setting of importance and "respect" for the music, so a forced attitude of "caring" can provide a setting or atmosphere in which genuine affection might be encouraged to appear. Consider the following example:

Maude White, whose real name is Whine, fifty-nine years of age and doing her best to look seventy, sits in her wheelchair and ponders her situation. Maude has two real troubles and a false one. She lost her husband five years ago. Her arthritis, although out of the acute phase and less painful now, has left her somewhat crippled, and she has no interest outside her day-to-day health. Her two sons are married and come to visit her as infrequently as possible, since they are well acquainted with her chronic condition and their wives are not too keen about spending any more time with her than duty and decency require. Her twenty-nine-year-old daughter Martha, whose real name is Martyr, more or less earmarked when a teen-ager to devote her life to the care of her mother, and having had a moderate sense of guilt instilled in her about any move toward independence or a life of her own, lives at home, her guilt sticking out of her like a handle that Maude can grasp and twist when necessary. The old lady is held together by her pattern of self-diagnosis and complaint, quarreling with doctors and manipulating her daughter. The only thing she is certain about is that she suffers. Her tendency to exaggerate her suffering comes from a belief that it's all she has. If she were really to improve, she would lose what has come to be the core of her life. Although she is not analytical about her plight, she is rational, and in brief flashes she knows (1) things could be better, (2) her methods of dealing with things (changing doctors, demanding more attention, exacting affection through channels of duty and guilt, etc.) are not proving effective, and (3) something is missing besides her husband and her youth.

Crotchety as she is all around the outside, inside there is a human spirit neither young nor old, needing, deserving, crying out for respect, and yearning to give and receive affection—a spirit wrapped up like a mummy in bandages of compulsive habit and conventional reaction. But human nature being what it is, those around her are prone to display their respect and spend their affection on people deemed more worthy, precisely those who need it less; and indeed, if these commodities were offered Maude in their pure and genuine form, she would be unfit to evaluate or receive them in her present state, the prognosis of which is very nearly hopeless.

If she were to receive affection she would be suspicious of it at first, and chances are that she would kill it at the source. For her to try lavishing affection would require giving up her domination-by-guilt, and this is frightening.

But let's set the stage for a miracle, an unlikely miracle, a far-fetched miracle, it's true; but then, what miracle isn't unlikely and far-fetched? Unlike most miracles, however, this one is possible, and it violates no tenet of logic.

On this miraculous day, so like every other day in her dreary life, Maude calls her daughter to wheel her chair out onto the veranda. The girl is taking a nap and doesn't hear right away, so Maude wheels herself onto the veranda, to be followed a moment later by her daughter, who says in the perfunctory manner of an actor bored with an overfamiliar script, "I'm sorry, Mother, but I didn't hear you, I was trying to get a nap. Couldn't you have brought yourself out here without calling, since you did it anyway?" Her mother's replying line is delivered with her usual skill. First a sigh, which packs so much information that words are redundant; "That's all right. I guess I shouldn't have called you." Except that the real meaning of those words is the exact opposite. No matter. The ritual is understood by both players. The daughter is now a battleground of annoyance and remorse, and the mother has eased her own anxiety momentarily with the satisfaction of having tested and tightened her hold on the girl. Bulwarked by the comfort this brings, she elects not to pursue it, and cuts short the daughter's next line, which would have been, "Any time you really need me, you know I'll be here. I do everything humanly possible." But Maude dismisses the daughter and sits staring at the hedge. Her mind traverses part of the arc of a giant circular rut studded with such landmarks as the possibility of her banishment to a nursing home if something happened to the daughter, the obtuseness of doctors, the mind-poisoning ability of her daughters-in-law, and the callousness of her sons. She is bored with this thinking, but what else is there?

One of her thoughts in the giant circular rut runs, "Does she [the daughter] really love me? Or is she just looking after me because it's the thing to do?" The thought flashes by, not in words, but definite nonetheless. And it comes from deep inside, beneath the mummy wrappings. It is part of the always stirring spirit seeking real love. It happens frequently and is usually followed by an equally inarticulate set of conflicting thoughts, the gist of which is, "I want to be really loved, but I also want to be cared for and not left alone or to strangers, and a sense of duty on her part is at least a sure way. I'd better not wish for something that might change things."

And then, like a stray neutron, or a chance grain of popcorn that leaps out of the popper and clears the fire, "I wonder if I really love *her*." This too has happened before and is not in itself miraculous, but on this day it coincides with her acute awareness of boredom and futility. She follows the thought, recalling from memory her daughter as a small child in happier days. Did she know then that she was destined to be trapped in a situation like this, her chances for marriage and happiness diminishing every year? For a moment the genuine love flutters and struggles to get out, and some of it filters through as sentiment and remorse. This feeling is one Maude has not had for a long time. It is not comfortable, but at least it is not boring, and perhaps this is the point at which the miracle starts. Her attention wavers for a moment between her discomfort at this new-old feeling and the feeling itself: a direct concern for a child she has loved. It could veer off in a split second through self-abnegation to self-pity and then to the comforting defense of self-justification. "After all, fate hasn't dealt kindly with me. I do my best."

But our miracle demands suppression of self for the moment, and it isn't too likely in this cauldron of neurotic habit. How many coincidences does a miracle require? As many as Huxley's monkeys typing a Shakespearean sonnet, if blind chance alone holds the field. But blind chance has two helpers here: desire and volition. At the deepest seat of our being is some knowledge that to "be loved" is not in our power, but to love always is. And Maude is bored to sickness with the futility of trying to get love without abandoning her techniques of exacting solicitude. So, for a brief instant, like going outside even though it's cold to get some fresh air, she ventures away from herself long enough to enjoy reviving a dormant tender feeling about her daughter. The mummy bandage has sprung a seam or torn slightly. A tear starts down Maude's cheek. And it is not shed for herself! But tears are not miracles, even that kind of tears. There is a long, difficult, and improbable road ahead to the kind of miracle we want to watch unfold. Feelings are not action, and all too often, tears substitute for action, because they represent the grief of lost chances, the bitterness of recognition of weakness and failure.

Maude has done nothing yet. She has not communicated to her daughter that she has harbored such a thought. There have been discussions of the subject in which both sides have followed the instinctive protocol of denying truth, and by building the words into massive edifices of self-protection, the mother and daughter have managed to shield themselves from each other and from the issue.

Maude dabs at her eyes with a piece of tissue and prepares to go back inside herself. But the fresh air was good. She stares at the hedge again.

That evening she looks at her daughter across the dinner table and manages a compliment on the food. Unfortunately, the daughter's reaction to the compliment is one of confusion, and is interpreted by Maude as a rebuff, which throws her back onto the familiar ground of self-pity and whining. The daughter is almost relieved.

But a seed is sown, and the soil it has fallen on is Maude's interest in attempting excursions outside herself, even if they are uncomfortable and sometimes scary. This is the base of our miracle. The next step in its growth is her idea that though she may never get used to the discomfort of disrupting her pattern of compulsive habit, she can tolerate the discomfort. She is "getting used to not getting used to" a situation. She may attribute this to her noticing (and admitting to herself) that though crippled and gnarled, the course of her disease has left her with less pain in this phase than earlier. She had at one time more or less "gotten used to not getting used to" that continuing agony. Or it may be that her vital drive was not atrophied but only bottled up badly by her situation.

It had not really turned inward to work destructively on itself. The mummy wrappings were not airtight.

She begins to think about Martha, and to be, at first curious, and then interested in what her daughter thinks about and feels. At least it is less boring than her circular rut.

In an atmosphere of curiosity and interest, Maude's random sentimental thought about her daughter now has a chance to grow and be converted into real caring. It also has a chance, by further drawing attention away from her own problems, to break deadlocks of futility and tension. That chance first showed up in the fortunate fact that she realized herself to be bored with her lot.

Does the likelihood of this train of events, even when bolstered by the reasonable possibility of a volition on Maude's part, strain our credulity? The possibility is the miracle. The seeds of miracle are everywhere all the time. The flower of miracle requires constant correctness of decision at thousands of steps along the way, or the painful recovery of lost ground after a wrong decision.

The obstacles between this elderly woman and her goal of improving her lot are formidable. Even if she were to change overnight, those around her may not. But if she can carry it to a certain level, the improvement in herself will have the seminal effect of encouraging change for the better, even in others. Martha's sense of guilt may never be eradicated. It's too much, too early acquired, too big a part of her to be amputated at this late date. But it's force can be, to a certain extent, redirected. It might be the platform on which she builds an ability to care about her mother instead of just caring for her. For love is like fire. It reproduces and expands itself. Martha may never marry, but her mother's (and her own) improvement will enhance the likelihood. Again, the real substance of the miracle is the possibility and the tantalizing fact that within everyone is the potential and the power to make improvements.

# CHAPTER IX

## *Myths of Love*

[1]

More has been written about love than about any other human emotion. There are so many definitions of love and apparently so many different manifestations of it that most languages lack the adequacy to deal with this phenomenon.

The inadequacy of the English language is shown in the fact that this single four-letter word is employed in a newspaper headline to chronicle a crime of passion labeled a "love-nest slaying" and by a minister in the pulpit to describe how we ought to feel about God. It has been called "the most overworked word in the English language."

In adopting a definition, I want to review definitions of psychologists, slough off the false feelings tagged by the word, and then try to find and trace the unifying thread that runs through the many different forms in which love operates.

Love, having its roots in the emotions, cannot be controlled by the intellect, any more than a steering mechanism can be controlled by a car. Intellect can analyze, determine expedients, calculate odds, and offer choices. But the emotions make the decisions. "Our choices spring from more imperative stuff than thoughts," says Allan Fromme. And Freud came to believe that a prime use of our rational faculty is the justification of these choices to ourselves in the eyes of the outside world.

Neither can love be called into being or annihilated by the intellect. Although the intellect can offer clear evidence that it would be better if such-and-such a feeling did not exist, it cannot turn it off by any direct means. Nor can it kindle love after finding that it would be expedient if that feeling could be fastened to a certain person or object. How many times have parents hoped that attraction and love could be kindled for a partner candidate "suitable" to one of their children and been baffled that nothing happened?

Through four basic types of love and several subtypes, not to mention myriad blends of all these, one thing is universally characteristic of the phenomenon: its obsessive quality. Once kindled, it "locks on" to the love object and focuses an anxious attention unremittingly on it. Where expenditure of other emotional energy shows economy, the energy of love is profligate. It overloads, so to speak, the filament connecting the lover and the loved object, and what spills over colors everything outside. To one in love the sun becomes brighter, the flowers and sky more beautiful with a special color of their own.

Although love is a basic drive, it is a very complicated kind of motivation. It is common in the way a human body is common, even though very complicated. We probably have emotional circuits or patterns all preprogrammed and ready to go into action when triggered. The characteristics are a tendency to fasten onto some sort of object; to focus attention of an urgent, anxious nature on the object and on the attachment itself; to suffuse the urgency and anxiety with a feeling of deliciousness not present in other anxieties and never absent in love, even during painful stretches of it; and to endow itself through conscious thought with a strong conviction that it is eternal.

Most of us have experienced the feeling of being "in love with love"—a feeling of overflow of the potential or the great desire to love, without having it attached to any object. But this is fleeting and feeble compared to the strength the feeling attains when an attachment is complete.

In the early stages of any kind of love, the urgency compensates for lack of a secure, firm bond—we go around shoring up the structure with timbers of anxious attention until the concrete "sets." The fire can be so fierce that it not only colors all other activities, it actually subordinates them to the feeling of love. A man may base important career decisions on convenience of access to a woman he loves: in an "affair" it may be to aid secrecy; in a marriage, or long-term liaison, it may be (and is considered appropriate) that his career is made a means to the end of happiness with his mate.

Nothing is as fickle as love itself can be. It appears as mysteriously as the light of a firefly. And it flickers out just as mysteriously. But while the glow is there, it becomes inconceivable to the affected person that it will ever end. And it makes it difficult to believe that it hasn't always existed. This is its "eternal" quality. "I will always love you" can be uttered with complete sincerity and conviction, even though in the mind of the utterer there is a clearly remembered procession of loves that have come and gone. *This* one is always different because the old ones are no longer the same.

A naïvely Victorian dictionary defines love as "tender and passionate affection for one of the opposite sex," going on to call it a "strong liking, fondness and a feeling of strong, personal attachment." The love described here is widespread enough to be considered normal, but the limitation to interpersonal and heterosexual attachment is unscientific and judgmental.

We usually think that the attached object is the source of the love. But Freud says that the love is really the attachment. Further, the kind of attachments we make and the kind of things and people we "attach" are the results of early experiences, and a pattern of behavior is discernible and to a certain extent predictable. Fromme says, "There are attachments that we develop out of desire and choice and others that we develop out of need and experience. The former have a conscious, rational quality; the latter, an animal and accidental quality. Love . . . is not some rare, delicious, incomprehensible set of feelings growing out of some special attachment to some special person. Love is that attachment but also any and all other attachments as well, whether they be to things or people, pleasant or unpleasant, new or old, conscious or unconscious. Our loves are many. Many of them coexist; some nourish each other, and some conflict. The future of any one love depends upon its place in the complex pattern of all our loves."*

Before examining the classification I've adopted, for types and subtypes of love, let's look briefly at some Greek words and Church definitions.

*Eros, philia,* and *agape* are three kinds of love pondered by churchmen for many years. Although the adjective "erotic" has taken on a meaning of purely sexual feeling in modern English, it is more than that in its original and pure form. Called the "love of the lovable" *eros* has been believed by religious definition (and the Greeks) to have its source in the object or loved one. *Philia,* according to a bishop, is "the affection that arises between people because of mutual interest or focus; an outside factor is its source." *Agape* is a love directed at someone not lovable. "We can say quite plainly and colloquially that Christian love is the business of loving the unlovable, i.e., the unlikeable," says Professor Fletcher.†

Although perhaps the original idea of *agape* is more akin to what we will later call universal love (in that to be genuine it must be a feeling of love for the unlovable and not just dutiful action toward them), the attitude of many Christian moral theologians has been that since a feeling of love cannot be commanded and charitable actions can, *agape* as a Christian duty is more a reality if interpreted as duty than if left to chance, as the genuine caring must be. James A. Pike said, "[*Agape*] *is not the best brand of love, either for the lover or the loved. It is not enough.*" It has the effect of "putting down" the person at whom it is directed. *Agape,* thus defined, falls completely outside the defini-

* Allan Fromme, *The Ability to Love* (New York: Pocket Books, 1965), p. 12.
† Joseph Fletcher, *Situation Ethics* (Philadelphia: Westminster Press, 1966), p. 105.

tion of love, and should not be called love. But at the heart of the Christian message is a pretty clear indication that although it is morally commendable to be just and helpful to your fellows, if you do all this "and have not charity" (that is, if you do not really feel a sense of caring), you're out of it. Whether the ability to care deeply and unconditionally about the "unlovable" is a cause or a manifestation of salvation is debatable, but a high level of maturity is marked by this kind of genuine caring even for genuinely unlikable people. It comes under the fourth type of love in the classification below.

[2]

I should explain as I go along what I mean by the words I've chosen to denote each type of love. This method of arranging them is not arbitrary, nor is it congruent with any system put forth in modern psychological theory, but rather it relates to the view of maturity (maturing) developed in this book.

The four main types of love I call sexual, affective, familial, and universal.

"Sexual" is very nearly self-explanatory. By "affective" I mean the drive that narrows and organizes emotional attention as the wave trains of a laser beam are narrowed and put in step. The obsessive quality is found to be more or less continuous in the emotional feelings of affective love, whereas it is much more capricious and momentary in the sexual. "Familial" love is a specialized feeling, with subtypes discussed below. It is partially atavistic, and a good part of it exemplifies empathetic provincialism. Finally, what I call "universal" love (not in the sense of being common to all mankind, but being a type of love not limited to certain love objects) is a feeling still definable as love, but directed without restraint toward all living beings, inanimate things, and processes of the universe. It is itself in two subtypes. It is rare, but it is not myth.

*Sexual.* This is listed first, not because of its universal interest, but because it appears independently of any significant level of maturity. Not even complete physical maturity is requisite, as Freud discovered. Sex, as he developed it in his theory, is a drive operating even in the very young. It matures with physical development into the complex, physiological process necessary to reproduction, but it is there from the outset. Much of the emotional pattern of the individual's future life is shaped by the encounters of this drive in early years. If Freudian theory is accepted, this kind of love is an element in every other kind of love, even when it is eclipsed or sublimated.

Looked at one way, the very foundation of the sex drive must be narcissistic. Literal self-love must be at the base of every feeling of love. We are told by psychologists that inability to love ourselves leaves us unable to love others. In sexual encounters it is impossible to be unaware of our own physical satisfaction, so pure sex has a root in autosexuality. If this autosexuality operates to exclude the more complicated sexuality that we expect with fuller development, then the individual is arrested at a primitive level. But the first subtype of the first category of love is the autosexual.

The next is homosexual. Although brilliant homosexuals have argued persuasively that homosexuality is not necessarily inferior to heterosexuality, and the homosexual community affects to look with pity on the troubles heterosexuals suffer (unwelcome pregnancies, divorce, etc.), the consensus among psychologists, even subtracting moralistic bias, is that homosexuality is a warp, an abnormality most often rooted in arrested development. We know that a homosexual phase is traversed during early adolescence and, if development continues, outgrown. It is nonproductive and, in this light, a miscarrying of the basic intent of the sex drive: to reproduce the species.

There is, however, room for progress both in understanding the phenomenon and adopting a more tolerant attitude toward it than is generally found in Judeo-Christian culture. The condition itself causes far less agony and disruption to individual and community than the cruelty of outmoded laws and widespread prejudice. If a proper tolerance could be adopted by the community, I suspect that homosexuality, once relieved of the pressure of disapprobation, would come to be regarded as less of a defect.

In any case, like autosexuality, homosexuality is a factor in everyone's life, no matter how normal he may be judged and no matter how heterosexual his outlook and habits.

Physiologically, we all have hormones of both sexes; we all have at least traces of both sets of organs and gland tissues; and we all have traits of the other sex in our personality and emotional makeup, whether a little or a lot and whether it troubles us and we fight to hide it, or whether we relax and accept it. The degree of disgust heterosexuals register at overt homosexual activity among consenting partners is very likely an index of fear they feel about something in themselves. In any case, a homosexual motive is interpersonal and represents, on the sexual level, a degree of empathy and a higher level of maturity than exclusive autosexuality.

Homosexuality has no need to apologize for the quality of its love. The idea that the homosexual is incapable of the higher feelings of empathetic response because homosexuality beyond puberty represents arrested development is completely false. Not only has some of our most beautiful creative literature and art come from homosexuals, but there is abundant evidence that interpersonal feelings and attachments among homosexuals can have the same level of subtlety, sincerity, complexity, and genuineness that the finest heterosexual love has. The authentic ring of love in the poetry of Sappho is a case in point. It is possible that the social obstacles to homosexual love may even operate to heighten some aspects of it, in the same way that obstacles to heterosexual love can intensify the feelings (e.g., Romeo and Juliet, Abelard and Heloise, Tristan and Isolde).

Where emotional growth and physiological balance have progressed through puberty without surrendering to arresting or distorting influences, heterosexuality emerges.

The curious interplay between physical processes and emotions is on some levels quite inseparable. The almost mechanical process of an erection (observable even in very young males) is not identical with an erotic feeling, which requires an emotional or at least ideational component. It does not require the complex feeling of love, but there is an emotional factor in "feeling" sexual. We think of it as a physical feeling. Technically there can be purely physical *conditions*, but all physical *feelings* have some emotional component. (This refers to the earlier contention that stimuli are not only registered but interpreted.)

Because the emotional mechanism necessary to the development of a strong heterosexual technique does not necessarily entail the kind of emotional maturity that carries potential for the higher forms of love, we frequently see immature people, quite heterosexually oriented but making miserable matches and botching up their love life with compulsive and childish behavior.

Conversely, there are people whose early emotional experience have stunted their development at a homosexual level, but who, in spite of this handicap, have flowered into emotional responsibility in nonsexual areas (and here I challenge Freudian theory in posing nonsexual emotions) sufficiently to establish lasting and loving attachments not unduly subject to jealousy, possessiveness, or sado-masochistic needs.

The sexual element in life can be called a type of love because it contains the elements listed earlier: it has a tendency to fasten onto an object (in autosexuality the object is one's own body); it focuses eager and full attention on it; it suffuses the urgency with deliciousness; it dominates conscious thought; and although each episode is relatively short-lived, while the heat is on, it carries a conviction that it will persist indefinitely.

*Affective.* This is difficult to conceive as existing totally apart from any feeling or observed manifestation of love involving other categories. In feelings for other humans, the sexual is either allowed scope or it is eclipsed (denied, held at bay) or sublimated (translated to other energies). In feelings for other objects such as things or activities, it may have its purest form, but even here, a good deal of sublimated sex may be inherent.

The so-called platonic relationships between humans account for friendships of various types. For a friendship to be genuine it must fit the definition of a type of love, though healthy friendships are more rational in character than other types of love, and the characteristics displayed are all of rather milder order than in other types of love.

First of all, there is an object: the friend. The attachment is not so exclusive as to preclude having more than one friend. Second, attention is given the friend—attention much more under the control of rational consideration than that accorded the object of romantic or sexual interest, but attention nonetheless. We may look forward to seeing a friend, and be somewhat aware of missing him shortly after his departure. If these characteristics were intense or bothersome, we could assume we are dealing with something more than a platonic relationship.

The "urgent," "anxious" nature of our attention to a friend is minimal. If he has a problem or is in danger, we may worry about him, but we don't hover over our *attachment* to him in the same feverish way we do with someone we're in love with. Where love has a delicious flavor, friendship is seasoned with something quieter, more prosaic, and of the nature of fun and satisfaction. This is the *philia* of the Greeks—a liking, which may not dominate conscious thought, but it exists in conscious thought form and it also carries the idea that it's not likely to change or come to an end. If romantic love is incandescence, friendship is merely warmth.

There are ways in which healthy friendships are appropriately circumscribed, depending on the needs of the friends. There is often a limitation of intimacy by tacit understanding. Usually this is a response to respect for the friend's desire for privacy and a need for privacy on our own part. The protocol is infinitely varied and should be tailored to each friendship. People insensitive to it can lose friends as quickly by invading their privacy through an unhealthy curiosity, or burdening them with sticky details of their own interior mess, as by withholding all intimacies in a formal aloofness.

Romantic love (or rather the romantic element in love) is highly obsessive. As an affective form of love it is difficult to imagine it standing by itself, apart from sexual and some oceanic elements.

Unlike the platonic, romantic love is closest to a pure form in the immature but intense feelings of a pre-adolescent for an older young person in what is called "puppy love." People who have never experienced keenly these early feelings often deny they can exist, but a nine-year-old can be so in love that symptoms simulate derangement. A nine-year-old can moon, mope, lose appetite, concentrate only on the loved one, make up elaborate fantasies centered around being with the other (which may involve no sexual feelings whatsoever), and on being confronted with that person in the flesh is so plunged into confusion as to gibber. Having made an ass of himself, a prepuberty swain is saved from suicide only by a desire to continue his fantastic sickness. Thus does the strange and powerful spell of the goddess of love first come into our lives. At the homosexual stage this same boy may at twelve or thirteen be "in love" with some hero such as a nineteen-year-old lifeguard, emulating every gesture and attitude and day-dreaming about him. In midadolescence, he will likely be back to moping about a succession of girls, this time armed with heterosexual techniques, including schemes to convert his fantasies to reality, but he may never again match the intensity of that first withering and blasting onslaught of a prepuberty infatuation.

Puppy love took an enduring and curious form as a concise cultural phenomenon known as chivalric love through the Dark and Middle Ages and into the Renaissance. Grown men, if such they could be called, yearned for nothing more than a chance to carry a favor (a scarf, a glove) with them into the lists, there to kill in pointless combat a man they didn't hate, for a woman they didn't know. Granted, chivalric love was often sullied by lust, with loss of life in the boudoir as well as on the field, but the principle, and very often the practice, was that the lover never touched the loved one and desired only to dedicate his life and honor to her service. This was not a sublimation of sex drive. It was a separation. The knight may have had his fill of kitchen maids and a gaggle of bastard children who would fare indifferently, or perhaps he had a wife and legitimate heirs. This had nothing to do with chivalric love. The romance, the fever, the obsession were all in a compartment that he was conditioned to keep airtight and that he dedicated to the object of his insanity.

Not all love is channeled or attached to other human beings. Pets can be loved, as can inanimate objects and classes of objects. Even activities and forms of knowledge and wisdom can be objects of affective love. Some of these latter attachments carry stronger evidence of the characteristics of genuine love than does friendship.

Many humans lavish real love on animals. Sometimes because of loneliness or childlessness or where a surrogate for human partnership is sought because of a need not to expend love on an equal where some reciprocal demand might be made, or sometimes where there's enough love in the makeup of a human being for extra caring, a pet makes an appropriate object of affection. Animals, like humans, sense being loved, and many a pet is not only fortunate but worthy of human love. The sad side of it is that most pets have short life spans. In one sense, genuine love expended on an animal is not inferior but superior to love limited to humans, since it represents, by crossing boundaries of species, a greater empathetic excursion—a more nearly oceanic outlook on the universe.

This cannot apply to people so fiercely protective of animals that they are callous or indifferent about humans. A lady I knew once said of practitioners of vivisection, "I could cheerfully torture those people to death." She was outraged that nonhuman animals were used for the advancement of science, but apparently felt no outrage at the idea of vicious and merely vengeful torture of human animals.

Love can be lavished on objects and activities. We all know hobbyists who are obsessed with their hobbies. If they are collectors, they are obsessed with (in love with) the class of things they collect. (Collectors who speculate and trade for investment reasons may or may not have an attachment for the objects they collect.) A characteristic of hobbyists who are truly obsessed with their activity is an automatic assumption that other people are as interested, or at least potentially as interested, in the subject as they are. A collector of moose antlers, who thought of nothing else, on being told by a friend that the latter had met and talked with Brigitte Bardot, beamed and said, "Oh really? What did she say about moose antlers?"

Sports activities absorb the attention of enthusiasts. I've found that golf is almost a religion with some golfers. Such golfers will tell you jokes about golf, but none that denigrate the sport. And they will not make light of their efforts or accomplishments.

Not all obsessive preoccupation with activities is limited to hobbies. Many professions are loved by those who practice.

Archaeologist Heinrich Schliemann is a case in point. The energy of his whole life was focused on an obsession with the Homeric legend and the ancient city of Troy. His heroic efforts and the success with which they were crowned demonstrate that an obsession need not be blind or self-limiting. But there is the same strain of fanatical devotion in such obsession that we find in the obsession of romantic attachment—the madness of love.

Schliemann listened as a boy of nine to his father's reading of the *Iliad*, and he determined to find the ruins of the ancient city of Troy. His studies subsequently lead him to an understanding of how costly archaeological projects can be, and to a belief that scholars had been searching the wrong areas for the ruins. Because his theory of Troy's location was considered outlandish by established scholars, he knew he would have to back his expeditions with his own money, and to this end he amassed a fortune in the indigo trade, learned ancient and modern Greek, transferred his wealth and residence to Greece, married a Greek woman, and visited Homeric sites. He had become more and more certain that Troy would be found at Hissarlik and not Bunarbashi. He found it where he said it would be, although at first he overshot his depth and discovered a city on the same site much older than the Troy Homer sang of, along with a great fortune in gold. His discoveries established him in the world of archaeology. His dramatic success would make improbable fiction, but then, truth is always stranger. What made it happen was his love of the subject—his single-minded devotion to an idea. I suggest that this idea was neither a need for vindication or recognition, nor the determination of historic Troy's location. Rather it was a romantic attachment to Homeric legend and the historic events that underlie it. He was in love with the story and the cast of characters (he named his son Agamemnon). Locating the ruins of Troy had the effect of putting him in touch literally with the love object. The obsession focused the attention of his whole life, gave his quest a sense of urgency and deliciousness, dominated his consciousness, and exhibited all the other characteristics of a love affair, including the belief that it would never end. When Schliemann died, nearly seventy years old, he still had the fever.

The roots of obsession, romantic attachment, and aesthetic feeling are all intertwined. They are not identical, but they are inseparable. When one rises, it drags some of the other two along with it.

*Familial.* The love we feel for people related to us is largely culturally conditioned. The nature of feelings for our most immediate ancestors, our mother and father, is compounded of need, respect, and fear and the affection that can grow with living together. This changes throughout life, the uncritical respect giving way to discriminating appreciation, and fear diminishing with decreased need. Affection and a protective sense grow as our parents grow old. This is the ideal evolution of love for parents. But often as the need lessens, the fear continues through guilt, and the respect degenerates into bitterness and blame.

Sibling affection, though conditioned through living together, can be strong enough in many cases to survive considerable strife and competition. Stories of brother and sister separated without ever knowing each other, later meeting and falling in love, but somehow instinctively knowing it was wrong and finding at last why they felt this way—these ideas are at best fanciful.

Our feelings toward our children are also largely conditioned. Aside from the instinctive feeling of love and desire to protect that is common to mammal mothers, love for children is made up of pride, wonder, and growing familiarity. Whether there is such a thing as instinctive father-love I don't know. I've never seen any evidence of it. A father's love for his children usually begins after they begin to show personality, and it grows and continues to deepen each year after they are grown. This doesn't seem to be an instinct.

Family, tribe, and clan feelings can be very strong. But to whatever extent they go beyond affection for the immediate family or those included in an immediate family circle (grandparents, cousins, etc.), they are totally conditioned and represent a narrow sort of chauvinism. Are family feelings real love? Some are; some aren't. If they represent an attachment, a real caring about a person or persons, and are not merely an excuse or platform from which to launch hostile feelings toward "outsiders," they can fairly be called love. Patriotism, in its higher meaning, is a form of love. Nationalism, on the other hand, appears to be the opposite. It is not so much love of country as using the country as a rallying point for hatred elsewhere.

*Universal.* This is a rare kind of love. It is very seldom seen, and proof of its existence is difficult. If we are to believe a few texts and scriptures, it has been attained by a small number of people, isolated from each other in history, and hence original to each, and in that sense unique. It is seen as a seasoning factor in some philosophers and religious figures, and some of it must factor in all unconditional love. In other words, anyone mature enough to love unconditionally any one person or object, has some feeling of love for all persons and things. In universal love the "attachment" links the individual to what he considers a "ground" or "essence." It is regarded from the outside as "mystic."

There appear to be two kinds of universal love, depending on whether the outlook is transcendent or immanent. The transcendent view conceives a subject and an object. The subject is the lover, the object the loved. The subject is the person. The object, in universal love, is the totality of all other persons and things, or a personification of this totality. The attachment can be as strong as in any other kind of love: urgent and anxious attention is directed to the object and to the attachment; a deliciousness amounting to ecstasy, we are told, accompanies the feeling; it dominates conscious thought and carries the conviction of eternity. In each of these facets it is, if anything, stronger than any other kind of love. It is truly an obsession.

The immanent view is more one of peace, for a very simple reason: The conception embodies no separation of subject and object. Here, the lover of the universe *is* the universe. The sense of wonder and the worshipful attention are replaced by a sense of participation. The deified aspect of this kind of universal love automatically includes the self. So there is, if we may believe the accounts of those who have reached this plane of understanding, less urgent anxiousness than sense of being personally divine. Apollodorus, on asking two followers of Buddha how they managed to maintain such serenity, was told, "Because we are gods." This answer appears arrogant to minds conditioned to a subject-object outlook, and blasphemous to minds formed in a tradition of a fear of God. Arrogance, however, requires an act of arrogating something to oneself, and if one is everything, there can be no arrogance. Blasphemy must entail a disrespectful or hostile attitude toward a deity, and there is no such attitude in the statement of the two monks.

Morris West, in his novel *The Ambassador*, cites a Zen conversation crystallized into ritual that shows the harsh, immediate simplicity of an idea at once too close and too exalted to be accepted readily:

"Why do you come to this place?"
"To seek enlightenment."
"Why have you not found it?"
"Because I seek it."
"How will you find it?"
"By not seeking it."
"Where will you find it?"
"In no place."
"When will you find it?"
"At no time."

The self-defeating goal, like the self-fulfilling prophecy, has scant affinity for logic. How can one search for something that his very searching will prevent finding? How do you attain something of which striving prevents attainment? Can you force yourself, for example, to relax? If you try, the trying is not relaxing. The dilemma is resolved only by a redefining of what it is you want. You gain knowledge of God by gaining the courage to do without God. You come on truth by abandoning hope of its existence. You see the light when you learn to live in darkness. These concepts are formed in Zen doctrine (if it is at all appropriate to link words like "concepts" and "doctrine" to Zen).

[3]

Obliquely, we may strive for maturity. But we can never enjoy the fruits of maturity by reaching out for them.

How do we redefine what we want? How can you set about to shelve one goal and concentrate on some other goal in order to attain the first goal? By what means does one gain access to the fruits of maturity without going after them? Or without appearing to go after them? Isn't this trickery? And, as such, can one fool fate—or oneself? Here again is the impossible process of "not thinking about turtles." And here again is a call for the second type of oblique volition—the one that requires action as unrelated as possible to the project.

One clue to a possible approach may be found in the existence of an apparent built-in safeguard. Few people will aspire at the outset to the level of maturity represented by the immanent variety of universal love. This "generic" or "oceanic" outlook appears frightening and has little appeal to those not already close to it. Thus a direct approach is seldom undertaken. If the sincere desire is simply to reach the next highest level of maturity, each step of the way, abandoning plans and pretensions of ultimate maturity, the project moves more smoothly. The office boy may find it unrealistic (perhaps undesirable) to dwell on detailed plans such as replacing the conference table and redecorating his office as chairman of the board. But he can realistically plan to become a mail clerk or manager of the stockroom. At each step he may attach himself to the next highest one and with care and time move up. When he is president, he may plan to be chairman of the board as realistically as moving from office boy to mail clerk. A man standing on the first rung of a ladder and ignoring all but the top rung might rightly conclude that such a step would split him in two pieces. This is why we look at the very mature and, shaking our heads, say, "I don't really want to try *that*." Even in the face of evidence that the very mature enjoy greater pleasures than we, and are immune to our troubles, we are *used* to our pleasures and our troubles, and we don't like trading them off. So we turn to other things, familiar, comforting things, saying, "Maybe for some, but not for me."

And that's precisely what we should say, and proceed to other things. The child who has just been returned to his mother after being lost in a department store is not likely to believe he would ever enjoy traveling in strange countries by himself. To aim tourist propaganda at him would be futile. This is why so much religious and philosophic literature is in parables, and why it stresses less the position of heights than the direction to be taken, a step at a time.

When a person loves, in any way whatever, he is expressing the maximum empathy of which he is capable. In light of this, all loving comprises at least in part the universal love of which we've been speaking, for it is the maximum empathy of which anything is capable. It amounts to loving life. Erich Fromm, writing in the August 1967 *McCall's* magazine, says, "Anyone who believes he loves a person and who does not also love life may desire, want, cling to a person—but he does not love him."

If universal love takes in everyone, it must include truly despicable characters. How are we to love a Jack the Ripper or a Hitler? Can we, should we love the child molester, the sneak thief, the bigot? Much confusion comes from failure to separate evil ideas, acts, and results from what we think of as evil people. It is possible to love any living person, even while opposing with all necessary force his ideas, his plans, and his actions. The benefits of making this separation accrue more to the subject than the object. "Hate is a weapon we wield by the blade." Curiously, the idea of separating evil from people is opposed by many. Let's examine the grounds.

First, a plea for a loving attitude toward "rotten" people is construed as condoning or encouraging their behavior. Second, to "hate the sin but not the sinner" seems to remove responsibility for evil-doing from the evildoer. This offends Puritan tradition. Third, a body of morality gathers strength from a community feeling of abhoring what is considered immoral, and hatred of those outside the pale of approved codes reinforces the codes. The hatred is also motivated in part because those indulging immoral actions are seen to be enjoying things the "moral" people secretly wish they could enjoy too. Fourth, compassion for evil people breeds apathy and undermines morality. These are the arguments. More cogent and more central to the problem is that hatred is an emotion more dear even than grief. This is why we clutch our prejudices to our bosoms like loved children. They justify our cruelties and provide a rationale for our dislikes. Try to restore a man's loss, but don't rob him of his grief. Try to comfort a victim of evil, but don't rob him of his hate. He will only hate you too.

Perhaps setting about to stamp out hate is an unrealistic goal. But hate can be redirected. If we compare it to guilt, which may cause one man to develop heart trouble and another to endow a university, hate can cause one man to shout at a civil rights demonstrator, and another to push legislation to diminish injustice. We don't have to quit hating. It's simply that we will benefit ourselves as well as society by hating certain things rather than others. In general, if we hate conditions, actions, and ideas, we are still free to feel kindly toward all people.

One more word on the idea that there are no evil people, no really unlovable people. If a Bengal tiger got out of his cage and found his way into a schoolroom full of children, and you were there, and for the purposes of the problem, fully capable of killing the animal; and further, if in your best judgment the tiger would very soon eat some of the children (and you) unless you killed it; and so, deciding not to let that happen, you killed it, your feelings accompanying the action of killing it might be of sadness for the beast, or indifference, or hatred. It is of no importance to the tiger. But it is very important to you.

A mature individual rises above reliance on hatred as a motivation to corrective action just as a mature society will rise above the official vengeance of retributive justice as necessary to crime deterrence.

*Love* an unlovable? A Hitler? You are not being urged to try this. Or even to desire to try it. Think of yourself instead. Wherever outrage is occurring over which you have some potential of corrective action, vent your spleen on the outrage. If this necessarily entails opposing, forcing, harming (or killing), keep your mind on the corrective and avoid hating.

Condoning killing may seem a shocking thing to some, even to some who believe in "just" wars and capital punishment. But there are very few people who would not take human life in special circumstances. If refusal to kill one madman or criminal would result in the certain death of one's entire family, not taking the indicated action is a decision tantamount to committing multiple murder. We cannot avoid "playing God." Such a decision is of a different character from hiding behind socially approved killing when one believes the ritual to be unjust. The spirit of the Commandment "Thou shalt not kill" is interpretable, in light of the moral necessity to minimize killing, as, "Thou shalt be the instrument of the least possible number of killings." This is theologically debatable, for it opens the door to preventive warfare and possibly, in loose interpretation, to euthanasia, and it implies and requires great purity of motive and soundness of judgment. The original blanket commandment—"Thou shalt not kill"—is probably more useful to social stability at this level of maturity. But the problem is that we abrogate it officially (with war and capital punishment) while condemning it individually. Escape from hatred of fellow humans can, in time, lay out a breeding ground for universal love.

What is the best love? I would suppose it to be the most authentic love. And if we are not ready, from a maturity level, to experience universal love in either its immanent or transcendent forms, there is a powerful and authentic love available to those who have achieved reasonable levels of physical, mental, sexual, and emotional maturity. That is the love between a man and a woman who have the luck to find each other, and the strength to nurture a natural love through a long-term liaison. In most societies, this is traditionally best achieved through marriage. It starts with attraction and sexual desire, flowers into romantic feeling, and ripens into affection and familial attachment. At every stage, it is a compound of all four types of love, although the proportions change with time.

The initial attraction may be sexual, or romantic, or in some cases platonic. There is some universal love (a love of life that spills onto the partner) and possibly a trace of familial love through resemblance to feelings for a loved relative or merely parallel affections.

In the Victorian mode of thought the attachment is strengthened through an engagement period by delay of consummation. (There is a quaintness to these euphemisms so gingerly applied.) This was the Victorian Era's method of controlling an explosive human characteristic. The fiction it built about marriage, binding parties to thunderous legal vows, brought to a peak a tendency through the ages to make the fiction of marriage real and the reality of love fictional.

Although a strong and balanced love can "keep" for a considerable engagement period if the couple is determined or conditioned to save themselves for the wedding night (few today would feel this way), little benefit can be seen from the test of a long, drawn-out frustration, the alternative to which is either eventual breakdown of the resolve, or premarital infidelity on the part of at least one of them. If, however, it is important to each to wait, there can be satisfaction in having proof of sufficient caring to tolerate the frustration, provided it is not too protracted. This Victorian idealism is still strong in the world, and within its framework, love compresses to a gallantry made more keen by the unnecessary character of the circumstance. If anticlimax is escaped as the honeymoon dazzle subsides, the larger but less flashy warmth of affection comes into full play and should have enough scope to make the waning of the honeymoon virtually unnoticeable. The affection need never wane, but over years of living together can change subtly into more comfort and less fire, with growing mutual respect, gradual increase of a quality of "dearness," a familial feeling through the bond of children, and a noticeably steady increase in the universal love component. This is an idealized relationship. Even it will have to weather storms of misunderstanding, thoughtlessness, inadvertent and intentional cruelties, weakness, other affections, disparate growth, and physical aging.

This is as close to "living happily ever after" as we are likely to get. Real caring can help keep growth and change parallel and synchronized into the same rate. In sexual activity, genuine mutual love puts appetite into concordant stride, and if desire and ability diminish simultaneously, there can be a peaceful sunset of considerable length. (The sun will not necessarily set as early as most people are brought to believe. Masters and Johnson garnered clinical proof of one man's potency two months before his ninetieth birthday, and the myths of menopause had been exploded long before.)

It might be said that all forms of love are oceanic in character. Certain psychophysical mechanisms shape love in certain ways to serve special aims: The sex drive gathers it into sharp, momentary focus and releases it immediately; the romantic draws on it to make a cloak of aesthetic necessity with which to drape a specific object for a longer time.

Empathetic impulses tend less to shape it than to draw on it as a source of feelings related to a love of life. Religious fervor, obsessive attention to vocation and hobbies, scientific zest—all these are related to a ground characteristic that smells of love.

We can define love as Freud did, as the attachment itself, or regard each type of love as something separate, but neither of these
views is adequate. Since there is a common flavor to all the forms,
they can be regarded as having a common source, an interior
quality and force, an underlying substance forming and power-
ing life itself.

# CHAPTER X

## *Education*

### [1]

The field of education—that is, the concept of education—can be considered to have as its aim the equipping of people with knowledge and techniques of thinking.

Educational systems, while invariably giving lip service to this idea, invariably pervert the aim into something they consider practical: the production of human minds conditioned to preserve an established order, to pass on the culture as uncritically as possible, to serve a state or an economic or political structure, and to force conformity.

H. A. Overstreet says schools are an anomaly. They can "help a student find his adult role—and end up by making him a complete reactionary and routineer. Or . . . help a student find his adult role in such a way that he becomes a liberal-minded co-creator of man's future and a person of unique powers."

Robert M. Hutchins, in *Learning Society*, writes, "Education is taken to be the deliberate, organized attempt to help people to become intelligent." The aim of education is to lead to understanding. It has no more practical aim. "It does not have as its object," he says, "the 'production' of Christians, democrats, Communists, workers, citizens, Frenchmen or businessmen."

Educational *systems*, on the other hand, are always supervised and approved by or within the framework of systems of government, "No education system can escape from the political community in which it operates."*

Ivan Illich, founder of the Center for Intercultural Documentation at Cuernavaca, Mexico, has gone so far as to suggest that "not only education but society as a whole needs 'deschooling.' " He has come to believe that schools are so rigid and stultifying that they are worse than a waste of time. The age-grouping, the walls and bells, the focus on teacher authority, the competition and compulsion, the credentialing, the irrelevancy of much of the curriculum, and worst of all, the brutalizing effect of a system that emphasizes the material while denying aspirations, are such, according to Mr. Illich, that society (and certainly the young individuals in it) would be better off with no schools at all.

Whether we do away with them or whether we keep them and call them something else, some system of "deliberate, organized attempt to help people to become intelligent" must operate in a society that embodies among its goals a good for its constituents. And Illich does not promote the abolition of education, only of schools. Access to knowledge must remain, and be extended to all.

It is difficult to educate anyone against his will. We can make available educational material. We can maximize the likelihood of its assimilation by various approaches. But if we attempt to educate by coercion, we will end up only conditioning, not educating.

This suggests that we should encourage oscillating between school situations and life situations, at least after a certain age, on the grounds that the motivation to learn will be more sound, and the assimilation of material greater.

The home, the press, and life all educate. They do so indifferently and are, if anything, more chaotic than systems of formal education. But their combined influence and their relevance are greater.

* Robert M. Hutchins, *Learning Society*, Britannica Perspectives Series, 1969.

The home may have been originally a device through which nature enabled life to break away from blind instinct.

Mammals teach their young. Reptiles do not. In the transition from egg-laying to live-bearing (ignoring for the moment the eggs and young of fowl), the young were not immediately on their own after birth. They required the protection of a parent. There is no need for a reptile to know its parents or its offspring. But mammal young require, for a time, protection and nourishment from the mother. The mother, in most cases, requires protection and a source of nourishment from a mate. This was the beginning of the family, the home. And in the atmosphere of companionship this situation provided, education came into being. The young emulated their elders, and in doing so, imperfectly at times, the door to experimentation was opened and some instincts began to atrophy. The learning process must have gotten under way with early mammals. Human life is freer of instinct than any other form, but we are still in a transitional stage, the outcome of which will be the domination of instinct by intelligence.

Young beavers learn formidable engineering techniques in beaver homes. There may be an instinct to dam streams, but the methods of cutting trees to fall in the right direction and the structuring of the dam and the beaver house are learned. This knowledge is passed on from one generation to the next, innovation introduced only through the feedback of accidental circumstance on environmental necessity, with little consolidation of gains.

The body of tradition began to grow significantly with the advent of human intellect and the speech it made possible, and entered an exponential phase with the invention of writing. The rate of increase of knowledge after the printing press came into being skyrocketed, and now, in the age of computers, it is explosive.

There is a fundamental—a qualitative—difference between the learning process in humans and that in any other animal. Because of the unique nature of human thought, realization of full potential for the human requires learning throughout the span of his life. Jacques Maritain said, "Education is not animal training. The education of a man is a human awakening."

But the home still contributes the principal shaping of human mental and emotional character. This shaping is more often poor than good because of the psychological unsoundness of most parents. Certain emotional malformations (e.g., frigidity in women) can be passed along in an unbroken chain through generations. Parents come from homes in which they too were conditioned early. But in homes where this early conditioning takes the shape of a solid but large (unconstrictive) framework of discipline in which to grow and develop self-discipline and independence, children are on their way to maturing and can rise above later deficiencies of school systems and unhealthy social pressures. There are too few such homes, themselves under pressure from social and economic forces that threaten to destroy them or, at least, render them insecure. The age of technology has proven particularly corrosive to the home. "The chief maturity-problem of our time is to discover how the home, under difficult and often forbidding conditions, can provide the experiences that will encourage the continuance of psychological growth from infancy through adulthood," says Overstreet in *The Mature Mind*.

Rich and poor and middle class suffer in different ways but with the same result—erosion of healthy home influences—from the effects of the industrial and cybernetic revolutions. Lack of privacy and silence; surfeiting with material things or deprivation in an age when the "other half" and how it lives is highly visible; lack of meaningful responsibility for the good of the family at each stage of a child's development; in the cities, too little contact with the earth, too little contact with other life forms, too much forced contact with other humans, too little of the father and sometimes too much of the mother—all these and other conditions work against the maturing process.

The most pernicious pattern in our culture—and it affects the home profoundly as well as our other institutions—is the belief, "You can't teach an old dog new tricks." We still cling to the idea that a child has a "learning period" laid out roughly from age six through adolescence and that then it is over. We smile at the occasional middle-aged student in a college classroom. We aim such phrases at young people as "You should get an education," as if an education is something you get once and then spend the rest of your life doing something else. "The formative years," to many, means from four to upwards of twenty. If the proper atmosphere is given a child at birth, he has a chance of extending his "formative years" to the end of his days. Maturing involves remaining "formative" for as long as one lives. When we stop "forming" it is because we stop learning and growing. Thus crystallized, we are less vulnerable to little shocks and more vulnerable to big ones. And we are less alive.

It has been estimated that some peak of mental activity is reached at about age twenty-eight. From there on there is a slow decline of the speed with which the brain functions. The maturing older person, however, brings to the learning process insights, experience, wisdom, and tricks of learning that he lacked when he was under thirty. Unless he suffers physical deterioration of the brain or is emotionally stunted enough to have withdrawn from remaining open to new ideas, he may learn faster and better than a college student of so-called college age who is profligate of his mental powers or unmotivated.

Parents set examples. Children imitate. If parents are seen to be learning, children will be motivated to learn. And they will escape the notion that learning is something to be dutifully and drudgingly acquired during a set time of life called "school age."

If the home is bad, is the child better out of it? Although there are individual cases where a court decides yes, generally the child is better off in his home than taken away. However indifferent the quality of educational atmosphere in some homes today, however lacking in freedom and guidance, humanity has not yet come up with an institution that does a better job of launching children down the ways toward maturing. No utopian scheme, no social experiment, no commune has yet proved superior to the domiciled family unit. Plato's "republic," Brook Farm, the Oneida Community, the Shakers, all proved transitory. Even the Soviet

Union is now careful to stress that all plans for the state education of the young will acknowledge the right of the parents to control the education of their children. In *Human Behavior* by Claire and W. M. S. Russell, the conclusion is reached after careful sifting of scientific evidence that "with all its present defects, the transmission of behavior through the generations by individual families is the most *progressive* form of behavioral inheritance that man has developed, because it leaves room for divergence and diversity. A progressive culture is characterized by freedom of parents to bring up their children, by the provision of facilities for education, and by interfering only when the influence of the parents is grossly or predominantly destructive. These are perhaps the best criteria for the use of the overworked term 'democracy.'"

In addition to home and school and street, there is the television set.

[2]

It is strange that children, having more active imaginations than grownups, bring less imagination to television than their elders. They look at it directly, and they see exactly what is there. An older person, conditioned by his life to view things in certain ways, will be absorbed into the drama, the ritual, the manners of TV presentations. The child is not so tricked.

I watched a television drama with my son, nine years old at the time, and realized after the program that I had seen what I was intended to see, and he had seen exactly what was broadcast. At one point he had nudged me and said, "The wall moved." A sick man in a hospital bed had put his head back on the pillow. I was intent on the situation at hand as the dramatist had written it.

I asked my son what he meant.

"The wall moved when he put his head back," he said. "It's only cloth, you know." There it was. While I was watching a patient and doctors and nurses, he was seeing actors and actresses and a set made of lath and cloth.

This is the way young people see all television. When they watch a political convention, they see the pomp and protocol, the bombast and sham, the people in the streets, the police, the barricades. Television, in doing its job of showing as much as it can of what is going on, falls afoul of criticism from young and old. The older viewer sees what he believes to be a hallowed political process for the choosing of candidates, and resents the disruptive addition of color elements, which represent a threat to that process, and which he feels thrive on publicity. The younger viewer sees coverage of a ritual he thinks is basically irrelevant and believes that too much time and emphasis are given to the details of that ritual and too little to in-depth examination of the causes of the discontent now pressuring it.

Young people absorb elements of their environment blotter-fashion. They tend to look on all broadcast material in a very real way.

I doubt that the very young are being corrupted by TV commercials. There is no doubt that the ambience of American culture is heavily merchandise-oriented. Advertising is skillful and probably is creating consumer desire, as is frequently charged, but the very excesses deplored so steadily are seen through by young people, who regard them as comical and who tend to reject the message. Television is educational, but not always in the manner it intends. What the young are rejecting is not the specific advertising message nor television transmission of any and all messages, but the momentum of the American drive that carried it past its original intention and resulted in the idea that "more is better." The dream that impelled the people who founded this nation to strive against religious persecution, a wide ocean, a wilderness and the harsh realities of life in its midst, the resistance of nature and people already here, carried to some sort of fulfillment the ideal of a life of material possession and relative ease. And now young Americans see their country still swinging its fists after its opponent has been knocked down. They wonder if means have become ends, and they sense a blindness in their elders as to what is now the job at hand. Television reflects all this, overtly and subliminally. In its old movies and new games, its commercials and its news, it holds a mirror up to the face of America. The young have clear eyes and are variously frightened, disdainful, or amused at what they see; the old peer at the face through the cataracts of social conditioning and are not dismayed by the face itself, but by the fact that the young react as they do. Many of these older people tend to blame television for the disorder. They are, in a sense, right. Television has opened its big eye and its big mouth and projected an indecent alarm, without proposing or projecting a remedy. I'm not sure it is in television's power or proper role to propose remedies; it offers no wisdom other than the cacophony of opinions unharmoniously sprinkled through its daily schedule from legislators, analysts, author-experts, and talk-show guests, and the implication of values set in tradition and taboo. The young, who indeed tend to see things as they are, bring no more wisdom about what to do than older people, and probably less.

I do not believe that the young are superior by virtue of their youth. But in absorbing the essence of an age they have the advantage of having no preconditioning to accept it in a certain way. When there is less hypocrisy in U.S. life (and hence, in the material transmitted by broadcasting) and more direct projection of true educational material, the gap between young and old and their assimilation techniques will narrow. Today, the older people who have accumulated something like wisdom, find themselves neither revered nor consulted by anyone of any age. And in the confusion, civilization itself drifts ponderously toward the rocks.

This is the situation television has lit up with its living-room glow. And it says to its viewers, "Here is the material, good and bad. Some of it is factual and, like yourselves, some noble, some shoddy. I have to interrupt it with commercials, because commercials are what allow me to continue, and you want to be told what to buy anyway. Some say I'm corrupting you; others, that I give you what you want. I'm not giving you so much what you want as what you *are*. Sorry about that."

Whether media and art are more influence upon or reflection

of society is an argument that has not been resolved. Those outside
the media and creative arts tend to support the influence theory if
things are going badly; the reflection theory if all is well. Those
inside tend to take credit if all is well, and to contend that they
only reflect when affairs are going wrong.

There are instances of pure reflection and occasional flashes of
manifest influence. But in a sense, all media material, whether
designed deliberately to influence (as in commercial advertising)
or designed merely to inform or entertain, has some influence
merely through feedback.

In times past the speed and volume of communicated data were
at low enough levels that rates of change were controlled and assimilable. Social shock occurred only with actual invasions and
epidemics, and certain elements of political stability depended on
selective knowledge—ignorance in the public mind. War could be
imagined a source of glory; sacrifices to Moloch, however painful,
could be seen as necessary. Bravery could be confused with eager-
ness to die. And what empathy there was could be controlled and
channeled to serve priestly hierarchies and patriotism to exclude
transgressors, social inferiors, and all outsiders. Idolatry and superstition were useful.

This ignorance-based control had a practical purpose. Given
the ignorance, the tribal communities, city-states, and nations had
to be structured for maximum strength and stability. If communicated data were sparse, then an organization had to form in ways
that required not enlightenment of the public, but control of the
public. And all nations, even the new ones, are in part structured,
out of habit, with materials not only no longer useful, but in conflict with a growing pressure of public awareness. Any structure we
build of flammable material in an atmosphere growing richer in
oxygen will become a pyre.

Old power concepts are no longer viable. And yes, we can
blame television for this. It may not yet claim the function of
education—to help people to become more intelligent—but it is
making people more aware. And this at the moment may be the
proper beginning. It can help people to become aware enough to

thirst for knowledge. And then it will have the mandate to move in the direction of supplying more truly educational material. In any case, it could not possibly do the job the other way around.

If it reflects the culture, in so doing it influences the culture. A man may learn from his shaving mirror that he needs a shave. But mirrors, except in fairy tales, do not say anything.

If there is a new order coming, if America is "greening," as Charles Reich claims, if there is a revolution and a youth movement and change at hand, in what shape will they come? Can they be anything other than anarchy? What will be their form and habiliment?

I can imagine a convention of feudal barons, gathered to discuss possible future forms of government. Someone, a fortuneteller, has just tried to explain American democracy to them.

Baron: Who would act as baron of such a land?

Seer: There would not really be a baron, Baron.

Baron: No baron? A king then?

Seer: No king either, Baron. They'd rule themselves. (*Laughter.*) Well, they'd have a ruler, but he couldn't do anything without their consent. (*More laughter.*)

Baron: Then there would be no government. You're describing anarchy.

Seer: It wouldn't really be anarchy. They'd agree on certain rules and vote them into law. Then they'd live by that law, or change it if they wanted to. (*Chuckles.*)

Baron: You are quite good as a jester, but very poor as a fortuneteller. And if you spread this kind of idea around among the lower classes, you are a dangerous radical. The dungeon is the proper place for you to propound this view of the future. Take him away.

The barons could not possibly see any hope of stability in a constitutional and representative government. And the idea of equality would of course be repugnant to them. How can we see the next form of the human community? We can only guess. Barring a return to the Dark Ages, which is always possible, governments will evolve, and most likely in ways that would be as different for us to comprehend as a republican democracy would have been to a feudal baron (we can safely assume he was ignorant of classic Greek democracy, since learning was for clerks and monks, and not the proper calling of a gentleman).

Possibly a black box in every home linked to every other black box and to memory banks of computer files of the world libraries and news sources with instant retrieval. Possibly every citizen a legislator, with no president or congress, and instead fifteen minutes a day from everyone devoted to government.

Silly? Yes. As silly as the U. S. Constitution to an absolute monarch or a medieval baron.

Our greatest failure in speculating about the future must be failure of imagination. Even a titan of imagination and scientific accuracy like Jules Verne missed the real flavor of the future times he wrote about. The flavor of his writing is that of his own time.

I'm told that some years back, when commercial jets were first flying, a ninety-year-old woman flew from California to New York. She had made the trip the other way when she was eight years old, and it took her eight months by wagon train. If anyone had told her and her parents then that in the girl's lifetime it would be possible to cross the continent in five *days*, it would have been too much for sensible, mid-Victorian minds. That she crossed it in five *hours* could not have been imagined. If someone tells me that I will live to have lunch someday on the moon I may doubt it, but I can't totally dismiss it as nonsense without thinking of the eight-year-old girl who crossed the continent east-to-west and then lived to recross it in 1/1440 the time.

Television is part of a technology that has brought not only increased volume of knowledge, but increased dissemination of it.

Not only the accumulation of knowledge necessary to the building and maintenance of complex technical systems, but the cybernetic branch of technology devoted to the transmission, storage, and retrieval of tremendous amounts of data have brought an explosive increase in flow of information. Awareness, in this sudden pressure of public exposure, is mostly confusion at the moment —a light too bright for dark-conditioned irises. It is part of what Alvin Toffler has called "future shock."

Every question about the future of man hinges on whether these changes, coming from all directions, are assimilable and to any extent controllable and whether we will survive them. Some of us want to know whether we can survive them unchanged. Some of us want to know if the changes they bring in us will allow us a potential for happiness. Some of us want to know whether any concept of absolute values can underlie new social and biological forms that may emerge. And a few ask if it is fruitful or necessary to seek goals and direction.

Alice, in Lewis Carroll's story of her adventures in Wonderland, asked the cat, ". . . would you tell me, please, which way I ought to go from here?"

"That depends a good deal on where you want to get to," said the cat.

"I don't much care where . . ." said Alice.

"Then it doesn't much matter which way you go," said the cat.

Does humanity have a concise idea of where it wants to get to? In the short run, it doesn't appear to. In the long run, the question has to be stated, "Does life itself have a direction?"

If television and other data-dissemination channels don't lead, should they?

They don't. And they shouldn't try. Because they can't. Leadership is ultimately with the individual. This is reflected not only in the failure of diplomatic expertise, but in the erosion of individual willingness to put up with a system believed to have lost its way— withdrawal from the system on what amounts to a mass basis. What traditionalists view as a breakdown in morals may instead be evidence of individual integrity carried beyond some tolerance level and forced to operate on its own. The breakdown is thus viewed as being at the official policy level. The more formal and stylized policy becomes, the more it shuts out the very values it may have been designed to serve, and the more it focuses on refinements of technique, intricate niceties, and expert opinions. Harvey Brooks said, "Much of the history of social progress in the twentieth century can be described in terms of the transfer of wider and wider areas of public policy from politics to expertise. Often the problems of political choice have become buried in debates among experts over highly technical alternatives."

Transitional phases tend to produce a good deal of milling around. When the herd has stampeded and heads for the cliff, if it is impossible to get the animals headed away from the cliff, it is desirable to get them to mill around until they all settle down. Not going in any direction is preferable to going in a wrong direction.

Popular disaffection is usually the result of diseased policy. Mass media contribute to the potential for maturity more by simply chronicling the disaffection than by commenting on the policy.

# CHAPTER XI

## An Instinct for Maturity

### [1]

Perhaps the most mysterious circumstance of our existence is that while there is the potential for maturity in every human, there is no instinctual aid to maturity. One "cannot draw on instinctive knowledge, for nature has not endowed man with such instincts. She provides for man's development up to the age of puberty, she endows him with the instinct to propagate his kind, but after this she leaves him to his own devices. Far from helping man to develop further into the harmonious and enlightened being he might become, the blind force of evolution has actually put obstacles in his way."*

Nature does not appear to be interested in much beyond our reproduction of ourselves. This is the mechanism by which nature led up to the development of her highest level of organization, and here she seems content to level off.

The puzzle, I believe, is spurious. Its solution lies in unmasking it as a false problem. It comes from a narrow view of evolution and of nature. If we see evolution as beginning with self-replicating molecules, then laying down and operating within rules of diversification and adaptation, and ending with intellect seizing the

* Robert S. De Ropp, *The Master Game* (New York: Dell, 1968), p. 21.

reins, then evolution has endowed us with little to aid in maturing. But if we take a grander view of evolution (and of nature), we see provision for maturing built into *our* nature.

Evolution is the anti-entropic force in the universe that has built everything from the hydrogen atom on up. Some scientists say it feeds on entropy; to others, it is negative entropy. And although it looks as if it may have been responsible for all organization in the universe, living and nonliving, drawing on some massive primordial energy, it is possible that evolution is that massive energy itself.

There is a force in the universe that tends toward ever higher levels of organization. So far the human being is the highest known level. (Not in the sense of quantitative complexity—we can at present build a computer with a greater number of memory banks or a greater number of mathematical functions or read-out faces—but in level or degree of organization, nothing known exceeds a human.)

If evolution has now devised a level of organization capable of taking charge of its own destiny, it no longer needs diversification and the mechanisms (natural selection, adaptation, experimentation, random change) of diversification. It will now seek to *converge* and consolidate the gain represented by this development of man.

In this light, we are part of evolution. And in a deeper sense we are the force of evolution itself. It has changed directions in the past, at different critical stages and thresholds. We are at one of these thresholds.

When alpha particles captured electrons and kept them orbiting, thus creating matter (hydrogen), evolution was at work, getting something organized. When, in the vast reaches of space, clouds of hydrogen gas fell in on themselves through gravity and formed stars, forging the heavier elements in their interiors, evolution was at work, raising the level of organization. When simple chemistry was born in the electrons' affinities for more than one atom, locking different elements together in a chemico-electric bond of compounds, evolution had found a new direction for the increase of complexity, a means of raising organization to a new level: the molecule. When dizzying heights in numbers of atoms per molecule occurred (tens and hundreds of thousands), organic possibilities arose, and in the organic soups of ancient oceans, an enormous number of blind-chance experiments took place. But evolution has been interested not only in repeating promising experiments; it has also been interested in consolidating gains and quickening the pace of repetition. Among the experiments brought about by great numbers of random meetings of units of organic material were some that contained within themselves the program for reproducing themselves. The self-replicating molecule came into being and accelerated the process of complexity increase. Evolution had taken a new direction and now concentrated on this form, gave it an oilskin and nutrients, and the single cell was born.

From the hydrogen atom to the single cell has been said to be a bigger chunk of evolution than from cell to man. When the cell had approached limits of complexity, evolution looked for the means to go still farther up the endless ladder of organization.

(Personifying evolution, as if it were a force or intelligence operating on matter from outside, may create a false impression. The tendency to increase complexity is part of the nature of the universe, the same as the force of gravity. There is no outside intelligence that "makes" the earth and moon attract each other. They simply do it. In the same way nature complexifies. This is what we call evolution.)

Cell cooperation was the next step. Primitive multicellular life took the form of loose and temporary confederations of cells which, for some reason not clearly understood, banded together when feeding grounds were exhausted and formed crude slugs, which crawled to where food was more abundant and then dispersed. Eventually, colonies of cells made permanent symbiotic arrangements and differentiated into muscle cells, skin, blood, organs, etc. The organizational levels represented in even the so-called "lower" life forms are stupendous. Atomic particle to atom, atom to molecule, molecule to organic molecule, organic mole-

cule to completed cell, cell to cell-group, cell-group to specialized organ, cooperating organs to organism, higher and higher it
goes. At each stage, each life form endowed with a drive to stay intact, at least long enough to reproduce. At each stage, evidence
that nature is at war with entropy. The increase of the random
element (the Second Law of Thermodynamics) means the eventual death of every living organism. Nature fought this with reproduction. At each stage (gravity forging the more complex elements, chemistry forming compounds, self-replication bypassing
blind chance, reproduction bypassing death) evolution struggles
upstream and always comes up with some new breakthrough when
a technique is exhausted.

Diversification was the technique for searching for an organism
suited to carry the main trunk of life forward. Competition among
the hundreds of millions of diverse forms developed on earth bred
tough, wily, resistant, tenacious types of life. One of them, a pri-
mate, was wilier than the rest and went off in a new direction.
His cunning gave him an edge, and he bred to increase that faculty. The brain enlarged, the forelimbs were freed to manipulate
his environment, and man emerged—to make tools and weapons
and clothing and conveyances and calculators and computers and
largely to dominate other species on the face of the planet.

Now he finds himself in the position of the dog who chased a
locomotive and caught it. What does he do with it? In a sense,
man has seized evolution and is stuck with the responsibility of
managing it.

Although this is true, there is another way of looking at it.
Man has not seized anything. He merely is part of something.
Man cannot contend with nature. He is part of nature. The works
of man—the electric motor, the Saturn V rocket, the Beethoven
Ninth, the Constitution of the United States, the hydrogen bomb,
the "Mona Lisa"—are all part of nature, as surely, as naturally, as
the web of a spider and the song of a finch.

But from an organization-level standpoint, there is a difference
between a virus and a lobster. And there is a difference—a fundamental difference—between a man and anything living that has

come before; man not only has more brainpower, but mind has appeared and has brought with it a reflective faculty that gives man not only the capability but the authority to take charge of evolution. In this he is not merely part and product of evolution, he *is* evolution. And that's where the responsibility enters.

Man represents a threshold from which evolution takes a new direction. Unfortunately, wisdom does not come in a package deal with responsibility; only the potential for wisdom. The acquisition of wisdom is part of the responsibility.

Maturity does not come with being human; only the potential for maturity. It's as though having been given a brain of sufficient complexity to give rise to mind, man is told, "You figure it out. If you weren't free to fail, you wouldn't be free at all. You're on your own."

There is an "instinct" of sorts for maturity in some people; a thirst, dormant in most, discernible in a few. People endowed with this thirst have the air of seekers, and it seldom manifests itself in intellectual guise. It is as though deep down we know it is now accessible. But it is not an instinct in the strict sense of the word. I believe this is because instinct was a device nature used while life forms were diversifying, adapting, and copying, and useful before intelligence came on the scene. Intelligence has little need of instinct and finds (in humans) that instinct tends to get in the way.

In the absence of rational mental capabilities, nature, needing a free field for diversification, in the carrying forward of increased organization found herself also in need of something to protect individuals competing for survivals. The instinct for personal survival was thus honed to a new edge. Cooperation was less emphasized than competition in a climate of dog-eat-dog. Symbiosis did occur, and this is a cooperation, but it occurred more in the lower than the higher forms, where strong instinct to survive carried the organism away from cooperation and toward competitive and self-protective habits.

Suddenly man, having developed all those competitive and self-protective habits (and needing them through his climb to dominance) is thrust onto the throne of the world, the scepter of intellect in his mind, and finds himself needing to trade his competitive, aggressive habits for cooperative ones. This is difficult because competition was bred into him, and since no other animal on earth is any longer a match for him, he turns this habit against himself. He must get rid of this habit or perish. He has his intellect. Why not simply use it to dislodge an unwanted habit—a now detrimental instinct? Instincts and emotional drives are not that readily manipulable by intellect, a newcomer on the scene. And nature doesn't aid her children directly in these matters, but she has laws that sometimes help. One of these laws is that useless things eventually atrophy—waste away and disappear. An unuseful limb or organ or instinct will vanish. Another law is that need tends to produce new organs, faculties, instincts—tools for coping.

Man, now in his transitional phase of having emerged rather suddenly from a field of fierce competition to one where thoroughgoing cooperation is necessary, finds himself at the beginning of atrophy of competitive instincts and on the threshold of the development of emotional drives to cooperate. Oddly, these emotional needs (being manifest already by the appearance of greater numbers of people who are less competitive sexually, politically, economically, less inclined to exploit their environment and their fellows, more inclined to live in harmony with nature) will be served not so much through the creation of brand-new instincts, as by the reappearance of much more ancient drives to affirm kinship with the totality of the universe.

Among early forms of life, before any level of real consciousness developed, it was less a drive than a simple condition—a state of affairs. Now in humanity, it will take the form of an ardent wish, serving the purpose of speeding the atrophy—helping to dismantle the unwanted and dangerous competitive instincts, still alive in man; and at the same time it will open up human individuals to a connection they've had the potential for all along. The stout will to survive long enough to reproduce, which served the ancestry of man through the long corridors of deadly competition with other species, built blinders onto human consciousness that forced it to focus on the necessity of *staying alive as an individual organism*. This is probably the origin of ego, the roots of which go far back beyond the appearance of anything like a human being. The need to stay alive as an individual will continue, but not as desperately, and not implemented by as stultifying a mechanism as high competition through blind ego preservation.

Human maturing is nothing more than moving along the line from competitive habits to cooperative ones. The way is open: We must move along this line as a species. We may move along it as individuals.

Nature never promises or gives any species more than a chance to survive, usually, after it has been given some special tool—sharp teeth, strong wings, night vision, etc. She gave us a brain—a brain complex enough to have crossed a critical threshold and given rise to a mind capable of taking over much of nature's work. Nature now steps back as though abdicating—not reluctantly or resentfully, but as a mother looses her hold on a child ready to walk alone.

The gods were angry with Prometheus, not for his theft of fire so much as for his failure to show cause that he and his kind were ready to make the sort of use of it that showed progress in a god-like direction. Now that we've stolen fire from the heart of the atom, we will have to show such cause. We already have an inkling of the punishment we'll suffer if we fail.

So now we are left to our own devices.

[2]

If we are on our own, what will become of us? Here are four views:

1. We will remain as we are. Man was not endowed with instinctive (organic) drives toward emotional and spiritual maturity because he is not supposed to arrogate divine attributes to

himself. This is the "If God had intended man to fly, he'd have given him wings" theory. We must stay as we are.

2. We will simply vanish. The universe is ultimately absurd. We will, of course, fail in any effort to develop wisdom or to direct evolution or to mature. Or to survive.

3. God is taking care of us. We wouldn't have the potential for maturing and the hope of maturing if it weren't already in the cards. Nature wouldn't have brought us all this way to lead us into a dead-end road. It will all come out right without effort on our part.

4. Man is evolution awakened to consciousness of itself. He will try now to conceive a goal, find a direction, and develop the will and strength to do what he finds he should. He may succeed or he may fail. The future is not determined, but it is determinable.

What is it that man reaches for in seeking maturity? Why the urge to transcend himself—his individual, special, limited self? Is it because he has come to know that he was cut from a giant cloth, that he is a "citizen of no mean city," that he is intimately related to something immense and is welcome back? Long before civilization it had given him the concept and thirst for immortality. He buried his dead in prehistoric times, and he began to worship long before he polished his stone tools.

Aldous Huxley said, "The urge to transcend self-conscious selfhood is a principal appetite of the soul." Baudelaire speaks of a "taste for the infinite."

Whether or not maturing is looked upon as having any spiritual aspect, it will surely involve some sort of extension beyond the narrow boundaries of self, some "other-directedness," some sense of kinship with other life.

If we are part of nature, and a capital part, then nature surely has a stake in our maturing, simply because we have such a stake. The absence of a blind instinct for maturing is only further evidence of some step forward—a move to a higher technique of operating.

[3]

In the areas where psychology and religion are congruent in their views of the human condition, there seems some agreement that man is in basic conflict with himself. Various religious explanations of this are dubious, but the evolutionary explanation has the virtue of doing no violence to reason. It goes thus: The brain developed as a control room for the nervous system. As sense organs gathered information about the environment—location of food, danger, sexual opportunity—something central was needed to sort out and evaluate this "outside" data and then direct the coordination of ears and eyes, limbs and jaws for the maximum benefit of the organism—to help it fly from some dangers, fight others, find and consume food.

The thinking part of the brain did not develop to interfere with or direct interior functions. No "thought" goes into the regulation of gland secretion, heartbeat, digestion, bile flow, blood clotting. Some functions are partially thought-controlled, such as breathing, swallowing, orgasm, excreting wastes. Most muscle use, on the other hand, is almost totally thought-controlled, except that skills (that is, repetitive patterns of muscle coordination such as walking and running, weaving, speaking), once learned, are consigned to less conscious areas of the brain, and play in and out of direct consciousness depending on how attention is drawn either by environmental circumstance or (brain-initiated) volition.

The determination of whether a process is to be conscious or unconscious rests on whether the function has to do with external situations (exposed to environmental caprice) or internal situations (largely insulated from environmental caprice). Decisions and actions about the outside world require constant evaluation of data, while interior actions can be automatic or habitual, i.e., "without thinking." So consciousness arose to deal with sequences whose outcome was unknown. One might say that consciousness comes out of ignorance. Again we see the null factor at the root of mental activity.

All animal brains, to the extent that they make decisions based on partial knowledge, are probably conscious. If there is something they can't know the outcome of in given situations—if they can't respond appropriately with an automatic reaction (i.e., an unconscious reaction), consciousness rises, stimulated by those aspects of the circumstance about which they must remain ignorant. We can't know exactly the level and kind of consciousness a crustacean enjoys, but it must be more than that of a virus. Consciousness is absent where life processes are simply chemical reactions. The presence of a brain implies evaluation of data, assessment of situations, and coordinated action taken following a set of choices—a decision based in part on not knowing. At this level —this threshold—nature developed consciousness. For a long time, up through the evolving, competing plant of life, both in its main trunk and its dead-end branches, the brain persisted and grew, and consciousness grew with it.

It continued to grow until another threshold was reached, and then consciousness brightened into something categorically different.

Human beings appeared. And with them, reflective consciousness.

They appeared a very long time ago by historic time. They appeared very recently by geologic time. They were different from other forms of life in a number of ways.

If we lay out a road a hundred miles long to represent the age of the earth as a solid body up to the present time, we can get an idea of how recently man came on the scene by considering that he first appeared about 150 feet from the end. (Man's mammal ancestors had first appeared about 5 miles back.) All of written history is within the last 12 inches of the hundred-mile-long road. The road continues to unfold at its rate of about two-tenths inch every century.

The giant reptiles had risen up 10 miles back and thundered along until 2½ miles from the end and then died. Smaller reptiles continue to the present. Mammals gained dominance over reptiles a couple of miles back. More brainy, more adaptable, capable of learning from parents, they showed early signs of replacing instinct with intellect, and set the stage for the appearance of man.

Hominids (human types) emerged gradually, but evidence so far gathered indicates that *Homo sapiens* (true man) appeared rather suddenly.

Most changes in the long chain of evolutionary life were sudden. They were mutations, which merely means changes. There have been so many of them that the bulk change has seemed gradual. There is no single "missing link" between man and ape. There were so many in the main stem from man back to common ancestry with today's anthropoid apes and so few fossil remains have been uncovered to date that most of the "links" are still missing. The change to man was fundamental in that a boundary—a critical threshold in complexity of organization—was crossed.

Mutations are constantly occurring in life. When the change is in genetic material (reproduction cells), it is more often than not fatal, resulting in nonconception or conception with failure to carry to term, resulting in miscarriage or stillbirth. Sometimes the change permits survival through this embryo stage, but inability to support life once out of the womb. In other cases, still rarer, the integrity of the organism is sufficient for the maintenance of stability through some kind of life span, but not adequate to cope with environmental factors. All these aberrations slough away from the stable, "normal" species type. They vanish, and with them the new characteristics they displayed.

But in very rare instances, the mutation permits the newcomer to survive and reproduce and to pass on indefinitely some trait that suits the line better to adapt or cope. This is what we mean generally when we use the word "mutation."

One of the things that cause these changes in genetic material is the disruption of some key atom in a complex molecule of a reproductive cell. This can be brought about by the smashing of the atomic nucleus by a high-energy particle such as cosmic radiation. We are subjected to this radiation at all times, and could escape it only by living in a lead house with walls several feet thick. A very great number of the atoms that make up our bodies are smashed in this way every second. A somewhat lesser number of the atoms of our reproductive cells are affected, as are a still smaller number of key atoms in the molecules of chromosomes—the gene material that we will pass on to children (and then only if the affected gene is in a sperm of ovum about to unite in conception of an embryo). So the chances of mutation are whittled down considerably by the odds. And even when the rare event occurs, the probability that the mutation will be any kind of improvement in the species is extremely rare.

It has to be the kind of change that will (1) survive both fetus stage and normal adult life span; (2) render the individual genuinely superior in some way, and (3) be the kind of condition that will be passed on—that will not dissipate in mixing with "ordinary" species traits, but dominate and create new individuals having the desired new characteristic. The chances of this extremely stringent set of requirements being satisfied are so rare that mutations of any consequence are few and far between.

But on a road of time that is being built at two-tenths inch per century and is now a hundred miles long, there have been many such changes in life—so many that they form a steady hum, a set of vibrations stimulating life into struggle, improvement, and awareness.

Most useful mutations, miraculous as they have been, were of minor type. A wider membrane between digits for better swimming (or in the case of the pterodactyl, between the forelimb and the body for eventual flying), tougher skin cells, sharper teeth, more versatile digestion. Many were of more importance: a light-sensitive spot that could lead to the development of an eye, the step changes that led to higher metabolic rate and warm-bloodedness, nervous system linkages that resulted in more efficient total coordination.

A very few mutations have been pivotal: those leading to self-replication (that is, the inclusion in the molecule of a set of plans that split off and provided the blueprint for constructing an identical molecule); the gathering around the molecule of protective and nutritive material enclosed in a membrane; symbiotic cooperation between cells in groups for the formation of an entity of higher organization (i.e., the birth of multicellular life); the mutations that resulted in cell differentiation allowing muscle, nerve, skin, tooth, and hair cells, food-processing organs, circulatory systems, sense organs, etc.; the appearance of the cephalized nervous system—a control room for governing interior functions and externally caused reactions; the formation of memory-storage elements; the appearance of a decision-making department in the "control room" and the first primary consciousness; the coordination of these last-named elements to form a brain and selective consciousness; the emergence of an animal not relying on specialization for adapting, and the potential brain growth thus allowed; the domination of reactive instinct by rational thought; the crossing of the threshold of abstract and symbolic thought and self-reflecting consciousness, and the rising of mind.

In all these myriad changes, the pivotal ones were not those that arose to meet a specific adaptive need—these would very often increase in the long run the organism's vulnerability to environmental change. The pivotal interior changes were those that permitted survival, but served no *immediate* adaptive need.

There is an analogy in pure research in science and in pure mathematics—which seek to solve no specific problem. The theoretical unapplied research discoveries have always been more significant. The geometries of Riemann, Levi-civita, and Lobachevsky are examples. Einstein did not develop relativity theory for the purpose of inventing the photo-electric cell or the atomic bomb. These things followed development of his theory.

Changes occurring in the stream of life that served no immediate purpose loosened the reactive bonds of life at each turn, widening choice and resulting in the kind of adaptation that instead of accommodating environment, encouraged the organism to *change* environment. Such surely is the nature of the development of intellect. *Adapting to environment is less important than changing it.* The most primal example of environment change is fighting. Demolishing a danger is environment change; flying from it is adaptation. Nest-building is another example of environment change; create the condition that will encourage an egg to hatch rather than wait until you can lay an impervious egg. Early life was more reactively adaptive. Those changes that I call pivotal, being less need-fulfilling and more random in purpose, led to the kind of adaptive techniques that were choice-oriented rather than reactive. Those changes were for nothing foreseeable, nothing particular—they merely didn't get in the way of survival. Out of the nothing (null) factor comes the climb up the ladder of organizational complexity.

The human brain didn't develop in order to allow man to dominate the earth. It developed for no reason at all, because man's specific needs for growth and survival could not be amassed. It could not be foreseen what environmental dangers would envelop man. The brain that developed for no "reason" provided him with the faculty of reason itself—the means to adapt by making choices and changing conditions as needed. The reasoning portion of the brain permits action. The lower portions permit only reaction.

The ability to change environmental conditions by a variety of techniques has been carried by man to high (and recently dangerous) levels. Environment change was so necessary in his early existence that a massive habit of effecting those changes came into play. Ecological stability remained unthreatened while man's numbers were small and his capacity for energy production was unamplified. Now he has the ability and propensity for polluting and denuding the planetary environment.

In view of this sudden threat to the planet's ability to sustain life (all in the last one-tenth inch of its hundred-mile-long road of history), is it still valid to say that adapting to environment is less important than changing it? Haven't we changed it far too much already?

Here again the uniqueness of human intellect has resulted in a unique situation for the planet we inhabit.

When we ask if we should change the environment, the word "should" brings in value judgments and moral considerations.

On the assumption that life (including human life) ought to continue, the only moral consideration properly brought to bear on the question of environment change is whether it is changed in such a way as to endanger or terminate that life. Of course it will change. But if we are to survive, it must not change in a lethal way. We cannot go on increasing our energy use and breeding greater and greater numbers of ourselves, leaving poisonous residues and depleting the resources of air and water on which we depend for survival. Right now we don't know how to survive without backing away from the kind of changes we have been making in the past century. And until we find out, we had best back away from them.

So far as I can see, intellectual assessment of the danger we're in is not resulting in corrective action.

Our rescue from the danger may come not from intellect (except as it is applied by a motivation to survival that will direct it); rather it will come from some deep will to live.

The will to live is a product of a life thrust that underlies both instinct and rational thought—a common ancestor, so to speak. Built into each organism is a drive designed to keep it intact, at least until reproductive age has been reached or passed, and usually beyond that time if it has a life span beyond. This drive has given rise to habits based on instinctively sensed dangers. If the organism runs into a unique or new danger, the danger may be encountered without fear, except for a miscellaneous aspect of the instincts that results in fear of the unknown. And sometimes even the unknown is not fearful; most wild animals can be approached at night with a bright light in their eyes. Nothing in the long evolutionary history of the animals has approximated this situation, and they remain curious but unafraid.

In the Galapagos Islands I picked up a land iguana and threw him into the sea. He was not afraid of me or being picked up, but he was terribly afraid of the water. He swam easily and quickly and scrambled out to be picked up by me time and time again and thrown back in. The very real danger represented by a human was not something to which he had been programmed. But something millions of years old made him feel he was in great danger in the ocean—some ancestral enemy perhaps long gone.

Humans retain a few instinctual fears. An example comes to mind: Anything that interferes with breathing causes panic. Underwater there is an instinctive urge to hold the breath, so as to avoid breathing water. This can be overridden by intellect, which tells us that air can be had through the hose and regulator of scuba gear. But in moments of stress, the instinct comes to the fore, and trouble down in the water means "hold your breath." This can be fatal. A lungful of air breathed at ambient pressure deep underwater and held on ascending can expand and rupture the lungs. It would seem that the sense of expansion in the chest would open the throat automatically in view of the fact that death will result from holding it closed. But never in the prehistory of human evolutionary development did a human get a breath underwater at compensated pressure. (At 32 feet in the ocean the pressure is doubled—twice as much air goes into the lungs to expand them to normal, as at sea level.) So if panic overrides intellect and the throat remains closed on rising, a human being will kill himself because it feels "right" to hold his breath. It feels more comfortable and produces less anxiety to follow instinct. We're not much better than the animals who can be approached and killed at night with a light in their eyes.

Nothing in the evolutionary history of man ever made reproduction a threat to survival. It was always the other way around. The more children who were born and survived, the more safety the community enjoyed. This has been true until quite recently.

Throughout the history of life on the planet, ecological balance was maintained by strong reproductive drives within a system of checks provided by natural enemies. Now, for the first time, the effectiveness of those checks is overwhelmed by man's intellect and his supremacy among life forms. He has no natural enemies but himself.

An anthropologist at the University of Arizona once told me that he believed that human warfare first came into being as recently as twelve thousand years ago, coinciding with the disappearance of a number of large animals—the giant bison, the mammoth, the dire wolf—which may have been hunted to extinction. When these were gone and hunting became relatively tame, humans began to turn on each other in groups. This view is not, as far as I know, accepted in orthodox circles, but we know that warfare has grown steadily more horrible in historic time, and it is not inconceivable that it had some beginning when man found himself with curtailed outlets for his killing instinct.

Champions of reason seldom entertain doubts that man will work out his salvation and his destiny by using his mind to subdue blind instinctive forces that could prove his ruination otherwise. They believe that the problems of war and famine and pollution and nuclear proliferation will be successfully dealt with through reason.

The human mind may triumph, but it will require more than the faculty of reason it possesses, which has already led to thermonuclear weapons and a runaway technology.

The reflective and intuitive aspects of mind, not so easily accessible as the rational, may contain the seeds of ultimate guidance for human affairs.

[4]

If you limit yourself to the financial aspects of the world of art, you will learn only the market value of paintings. The aesthetic element (which is what art is about) has much to do with the market value of paintings, but you will never enter into an apprehension or appreciation of this as long as you limit yourself to fiscal techniques of dealing with art. In the same way, the reasoning and intuitive aspects of human mental makeup are intimately related, but techniques of reason are not by themselves sufficient for judging the whole interior picture of man.

The trouble is that we have no techniques other than reason with which to work. To fall back on instinct would be a giant step in reverse. And the "techniques" of religion and mysticism are hazy and often self-contradictory.

Where we need to look is in the nature of the breakthrough represented by the appearance in the world of man and his mind. In what ways is the threshold of human emergence similar to other thresholds that evolution has crossed, and in what ways is it different?

Each pivotal point in evolution represented a speeding up of the evolutionary pace, a diminishing of interplay of blind forces, a consolidation of gains, a move toward self-activation, an increase of awareness. The threshold to *Homo sapiens* satisfies all these characteristics. Its uniqueness lies in the appearance for the first time of a self-consciousness, a reflective awareness—not merely linear increase of awareness, but a qualitatively different kind of awareness that shines a light back toward its roots. This unique property of mind reintroduces the potential for conscious kinship with the universe—primal forces that impel life in its thrust toward ever-greater complexity. This property, when sensed deeply by greater and greater numbers of people, can motivate humanity to fit into the world as the mind of evolution itself and thus find its destiny. This property can put reasoning power to proper employment and resolve the basic conflict man suffers now from his top-heavy reliance on and preoccupation with the rational side of his mind.

The next step forward for man will probably not come through sudden mass enlightenment but from the steady increase in numbers of humans aware of the potential in the intuitive and self-reflective part of their minds. This movement is under way. It is not anti-intellectual but rather nonintellectual. It shows up in the desire to experiment (communes, drugs, encounter experiences, etc.). It shows up in rejection of war, fashions, and sterile values. It shows up in the thirst for honesty, an abhorrence with the confusing games and rituals of middle-class morality. But it shows up in steadily increasing numbers of people whose life style does indeed constitute a threat to the status quo. They feel that if the status quo is killing us, threatening it is not a bad thing, even if what replaces it is unknown. Fluidity is the main characteristic of this new type.

A block of ice can be warmed from absolute zero up to 32° Fahrenheit, which is its melting point. At this threshold it changes to liquid. At sea-level pressure the water can be heated to 212° Fahrenheit, where it changes again, to steam. Water is not merely warmer than ice, it is fundamentally different in property from ice. Steam is not merely hotter than water, it is fundamentally different from water.

When the ice reaches 32° it does not continue to increase in temperature but stays the same while releasing more and more of its molecules from its surfaces in the form of water (which will rise steadily in temperature from 32°).

To a limited extent, human societies (civilization) may represent blocks of ice that will not progress in enlightenment en masse beyond a certain level but which, when heated up in the course of evolutionary progress, will throw off more and more "molecules" of fluidly independent individuals. New rules, a higher morality, may bind them to a certain behavior in a social continuum of an unimagined kind, perhaps with no framework at all. (Traditionalists display considerable alarm at this kind of suggestion, but it is not unthinkable.) In the frame of reference of rule by priests or kings, democracy is simply anarchy. In the frame of reference of a representational democracy, the kind of society forged by big numbers of fluidly independent people might appear anarchic.

A human mind—human consciousness—is not merely more complex than animal consciousness. It is fundamentally different, having crossed a critical threshold. This threshold is what separates reflective thought from mere thought. An animal knows. A man knows that he knows.

In human ancestry, ancient evolutionary needs were served by a brain whose complexity was below the critical threshold. Once this boundary was crossed by the brain, bringing with it abstract thought, awareness of mortality, the uses of symbolism, names and labels, concepts of ownership and justice, logic and art and worship, and the capacity to make massive changes in his environment and himself—once this great potential arose and man embarked on erecting the physical and social structures suddenly possible, he allowed an eclipse of some ancient aspects of his life. The light of this new mind is so dazzling, turned up full, that some deep inner glows important to our kinship with the world are forgotten or denied. We have become alienated from some truth about ourselves. And this is why we are in basic conflict with ourselves. The existence of religions is one evidence of our alienation. The memory is dimly there, but all we feel is that we have somehow lost the way.

There is no basic incompatibility of human mind and world mind, but neither is there any instinctual guarantee of refusion of them—any automatic natural mechanism for guiding the efforts we make to re-establish ourselves in the world. And the mind itself, dazzled by its own shininess, seems unmotivated.

A man needing physical exercise cannot sit in a study and get it from books—not even if he consumes whole libraries on the subject. He can use the books and his ability to read to find and decide on a program of exercise best suited to his needs, but then he must put down the books and leave the study and start exercising.

In the same way, mankind, now in need of refitting himself into a world he is endangering (and in doing so, endangering himself), is in need of readopting the view that he is part of nature rather than an alien dropped in from somewhere outside to conquer and subdue nature, and he cannot accomplish all this merely by increasing the pressure and pace of his manipulating habits. He cannot "technologize" his way to re-establishing his kinship with nature. Although he need not turn his back on technology nor abandon the marvels he has made—they can be useful in communicating and educating, storing knowledge, reducing pain and prolonging life, expanding human horizons, and exploring other realms—he must not invest in them such faith that they become ends in themselves. The main aim must be useful employment of these techniques and not idolatry.

We have fashioned a marvelous ladder for climbing out of the pit. It is so marvelous that we stay in the pit to embellish the ladder and marvel at it.

Science is, of course, marvelous. It is the product of our brain, which is also marvelous. But, having marveled, let us move on, because these things in themselves will no more save us than a tractor will plow a field by itself. Until it is mounted by a driver, it will just stand there being marvelous.

This awe-stricken view of "science" both gave rise to and subsequently reinforced a scientific determinism that has, in the view of Alfred North Whitehead, taken the role of Fate in the Greek Tragedy. He wrote in 1925 that the great tragedies of modern times were the scientists "with their vision of fate, remorseless and indifferent, urging an incident to its inevitable issue. . . . This remorseless inevitableness is what pervades scientific thought. The laws of physics are the decrees of fate." Of course, since 1925 work in nuclear mechanics has undermined some of the determinism and loosened the machinery of the universe a bit, but the "fateful" view of nineteenth-century science persists and has its home now in political systems and the popular mind.

We need now to shake ourselves from this paralysis of will, to name a goal, to find a direction. All this is not unknown to man. Very deep in our awareness is the recurring (and disturbing) thought of what we must do. Man sits like a drunk on the shore of a rising river. Deep inside he knows he'll have to move, but he lacks the will to do so. He has the knowledge and the energy, although he imagines deep discomfort in exerting it, and so he dreams and hopes foggily that some miracle will cause the water to recede before it gets to him.

The purpose of all this analogy is not merely to raise another cosmic alarm. (I tend to believe that the drunk has a good chance of being roused to real action when the water gets to him— that he will not drown.) The thesis of this essay is that it is possible and desirable for individuals to set themselves on a path of maturing that will bring great reward and at the same time contribute to setting the whole human species on a parallel cosmic path. Further, that unless it happens on an individual level, it will not happen. No legislation, no law enforcement (however sound the law), no courts, no dispensations to the poor and ignorant, no school system will accomplish the task that faces humanity.

The threshold has been crossed. The change has brought conflict inside man himself and with his environment. But it has also brought the potential for more than salvation. Man's first task at hand may be to back away from dangers he has created, but there is then the brighter task of helping the universe unfold itself.

Perception and cooperation with cosmogenesis is the occupation of man on earth. "*Love of evolution*: a phrase that was meaningless a mere fifty years ago; and yet an expression of the only psychic factor capable, it would seem, of carrying to term the effort of planetary self-arrangement on which depends the cosmic success of mankind." (Teilhard de Chardin, *Activation of Energy*.)

René Dubos, in *The Willed Future*, writes, "Science, it is said, cannot provide social goals because its values are intellectual, not ethical; once social goals have been selected by non-scientific criteria, science can determine the best way to proceed. Yet it is probable that science can help in formulating values, and thus in setting goals, by making man more aware of the consequences of his actions."

I submit that science can help only obliquely in the formulating of values. Science brought nuclear fission to reality and provided man with such a traumatic experience in Hiroshima and Nagasaki that he may have resolved never to detonate another bomb of this type against his fellows. I suppose that science "helped" here in a way. More to the point, but still obliquely, science has made possible rapid and wide communication of information. This too can help, thus "making man more aware of the consequences of his actions." But whatever is communicated through these channels, it will ultimately be a nonscientific value-set that has moved us toward the successful solution of our problems.

Science is the product of our fascinating mind. We cannot look to it to tell us what to do. We must tell *it* what to do. This is part of our conflict with ourselves. We worship our creatures as though they had created us. Science is to be used, not worshiped.

Again the null factor comes into play. Precisely what science cannot do is what may awaken us to what we must do.

[5]

So many concepts of maturity in humans center on accommodation. Some professional psychological attitudes and most public ideas about maturity stress factors of accommodation with such terms as adapting, conforming, and adjusting.

Since it is acknowledged that man cannot be separated from his social and physical environments, and these are known to be changing and imperfect, the ability to adapt to them must play a tricky part in maturing.

The pitfall is in assuming that the highest aim of the maturing process is to "fit in" with a given condition in society or nature. It is important to *be able* to fit in where deemed expedient or compatible with conscience or necessary to minimal comfort, and developing adaptive techniques and habits of cooperation is pertinent to moving along a track of maturing, but none of these can be ends in themselves, or the maturing process levels off and stops.

W. H. Cowley says, "Mature or integrated people are not 'adjusted' people. They are people who are intelligently about the work of ordering life and harmonizing it on an ever higher scale of human excellence. They are not conformists; they are reconstructionists." Adapting and conforming in the mature person are not compulsive. Adjustment can be consciously used —it is not automatically needed. (Nor is it habitually avoided. This can be compulsive also.) "Life is not so much a matter of the adjustment to problems, but one of the *adjustment to having problems*."

[6]

To approach the subject of emotional maturity from the operational point of view, rather than from the ideal or moralistic one, limits us to exploring what the individual is capable of doing. But beyond a certain point, it may be impossible to treat human maturing as a scientific idea devoid of judgmental values.

"We have no quantitative measures for estimating a person's state of maturity," writes Dr. Carl Binger of Harvard, "but we know something about the norms of human behavior. The methods of science are analytical and in general, its tools are not those that lead to synthesis."

The scientific method can, however, enter the spectrum of maturity at arbitrary points, and point out relative maturity among given individuals and types and against the known norms of human behavior. One need not be a scientist to establish rough criteria for comparing different humans on a scale of maturity.

Common-sense judgments will fail in the face of deceptive behavior imitative of mature traits (and even then, prolonged exposure can betray an impostor). Scientific method will fail only in dealing with persons of sufficient maturity to place them far outside the norms.

But it is not impossible to extrapolate both the common sense and scientific direction of maturing and then to follow it for distances, testing against some philosophic concepts of human potential and destiny.

We continue now with the traits of the relatively mature human adult. Child development is a special field, and we will assume that our adult has traversed that phase with safety and with the result that he has become noticeably mature and that he stands out in this way against the community as being in a fairly small top percentage. (Against the definitions I've assumed, most of the human community fails to mature.)

We've seen the mature person as able to "adjust" to his surroundings, but to be in command of the technique, and to withstand the pressures and frustrations of deliberately not adjusting when his integrity demands refusal (for example, he would brook the wrath of a lynch mob rather than go along with its project).

The self-actualizing aspect of this use of conformity came late to psychoanalytic theory. There is much determinism in Freud's original view of the ego caught between two tyrants: the superego (a conditioned conscience) and the id (raw animal drives). Little room was left for a creative force to impel toward ever-higher maturity. Freud's ego could at best maintain a shaky balance— an uneasy truce between these powers that pressed on it. Allport sought a way out of the dilemma by proposing an ego ideal. "Certainly a man is not mature unless he respects the codes of the society wherein he lives, acts with good taste and abides by the laws, suffering pangs of conscience when he violates the rights of others and when remiss in his prescribed duties. But is this activity of the Super-Ego all there is to the 'higher nature' of a man? Left to itself the Super-Ego would produce a personality completely caked with custom and shackled by tribal mores. Conventionality is not the same as maturity.

"The genuinely mature person has an Ego-ideal as well as a Super-Ego. . . . The Ego-ideal . . . is the plan of the developed personality for defeating, by transcending, both the unsocialized urges of the Id and the dullness of the Super-Ego, leading thereby to a new level of personal freedom and to maturity."†

Herbert Spencer, perhaps reflecting an attitude of his time, gave his famous definition of life in 1864 in *Principles of Biology*. He called it "the continuous adjustment of internal to external

† Gordon W. Allport, *Personality: A Psychological Interpretation* (New York: Holt, 1937).

relations." This has suggested for a century that people's lives can be "adjusted" by helping or forcing them to conform to a status quo. Both John Dewey and William James had doubts about the continuing desirability of this concept, but their reaction to it implied a stress on its opposite: Dewey pointed out that the Plains Indians accepted a status quo of nature and did little about it, standing still culturally thereby. Then, he said, "A civilized people enters upon the scene. . . . It introduces irrigation; it searches the world for plants and animals that will flourish under such conditions; it improves, by careful selection, those which are growing there. As a consequence, the wilderness blossoms as a rose. The savage is merely habituated; the civilized man has habits which transform the environment."

Aside from putting the Indian in a poor light (partly through an inaccuracy: the Hohokam Indians of southern Arizona had an irrigation system in some ways more sophisticated than what is there now), Dewey implies strongly that civilized man is superior to the "savage" because he "transforms the environment." There is something to be said for the wisdom of adjustment in light of the dangers now posed by such transformation.

The point is that both in the individual and in the societies built by individuals, steady conformity or continuous nonconformity are alike evil.

Maturity carries an ability to be selective about conforming. This ability has a root down near the source of life itself, for nature learned a long time ago to give its animals some freedom in choosing when to fight and when to run—when to change the immediate environment and when to adapt. This primal judgment must be related to (perhaps it is the ancestor of) Allport's ego ideal which denies the tyranny of both the superego (forcing conformity) and the id (demanding gratification of raw urges) by transcending and defeating them. The ego ideal is the autonomy and self-generating mechanism of the mature person.

Accommodation, conformity, adjustment, adaptation. Whatever we call it, it is useful and necessary, but it must be selectively employed, sometimes deliberately withheld by, a self-creating, maturing human, whose sources of morality are necessarily deeper than the mores and conventions of his society.

At every turn along the road of maturity there are what seem at first to be contradictions—contradictions resolved by backing away a step and viewing the process from a deeper level.

*The more mature person is generally happy, despite a penetrating awareness of reality.*

Most human happiness is rooted in delusion and shielded from danger by defenses put up early in life, blinders to reality. How can happiness come from awareness of reality?

The answer is that happiness does not "come from" awareness of any kind, any more than awareness "comes from" happiness of any kind. To be happy in the face of a high degree of awareness of reality requires a special way of regarding oneself and one's place in the world. If it makes us unhappy not to be universally admired, we'd better keep some blinders on, because we aren't. If we are made unhappy by being shorter, older, heavier, weaker, taller, more timid, less significant, less beautiful, or more dependent than we'd like to be, we'd better keep handy a pair of distorting lenses if we are to have even moments of ease. Some of these conditions are changeable, some aren't. But the unhappiness lies in the divergence between what we imagine we are and ought to be, and what a "penetrating awareness" of reality shows us really to be. Two ways of preserving happiness are: (1) to blind ourselves effectively to that reality and focus on an artificial idea of how we are seen by others, or (2) to abandon the demand to be taller, younger, trimmer, stronger, bolder, and more important, beautiful, and independent than we, in fact, are.

But can we "adjust" in this manner without giving up all progress? And can we do this and retain any sense of security, any internal stability? Wouldn't tearing away the blinders create such emotional havoc that we'd lose not only happiness but health? Yes, it would. Psychiatry has an answer and a technique for helping people whose happiness and means of coping with life are severely limited by emotional stunting and warping. Although most people haven't the money or time (or real need) for psychiatric consultation, in that they manage to make out in life one way or another, still, most people never rise above the threat of ongoing unhappiness caused by the divergence of what they imagine they need to be happy and what they are in reality. Since they are not psychotic (i.e., they are not out of touch with reality), they can't help sensing this divergence and being unhappy. This is one type of neurosis, and I think almost no one is totally free of it.

Does the more mature person escape this problem by accepting exactly what he is and resigning himself to it, giving up any hope of self-improvement? Does he merely "adjust"? Almost the opposite is true. The more mature person does accept the fact *that he is what he is*, but he does not adjust to it; he moves to improve himself in areas that are, first, realistically open to improvement, and second, that do not merely serve vanity (which is totally concerned with what others think). He seeks improvement in areas more under his control and more pertinent to real growth: the increase of autonomy, the increase of stability of interior organization, more spontaneity, greater efficiency of integration of new information, increased tolerance of frustration, deeper insights, wider extension of self.

Maturity opens the door from self outward to a limitless world. Immaturity defends self; neurotic immaturity defends only a false image of self—very limited targets, offering little chance of growth.

The second apparent contradiction is in the idea that *the more mature person is able to plan for the future*. This is reasonable—except that plans seldom go according to plan. This is a major source of frustration. And since the mature human should suffer less from frustration than the immature one, he would best do less planning.

The paradox is resolved by realizing that although the mature person *suffers* less from frustration than the immature, he *undergoes* much more frustration.

Inability to tolerate frustration results in suffering from it. There are two possible outcomes from an immature encountering of frustration: (1) outright suffering, or (2) retreat from the project that caused the frustration. Frustration merely means a thwarting or blocking. Whether one suffers from it depends on the person, not the circumstance; the suffering is not built into the frustration. This says something about the nature of planning.

The mature approach to planning involves a great deal of flexibility. And here intelligence is an indispensable ingredient. Contingencies must be provided for. Momentary compromise, alternate routes, deferred product, possible modified end-results, or even failure must be foreseen and acceptable. There will be frustration at every step, even in a successful project, but freedom from the suffering it can cause depends upon inner security independent of specific successes and failures. This inner security in turn comes from continued growth in spontaneity, stability, insights, and the extension of the self spoken of earlier. All these things, it should be noted, are dynamic processes. The maturing person comes more and more to regard himself—his self—not as a thing, but as a process. This process goes on continuously, an unfolding, a becoming. It touched the physical organism in which his animal consciousness centers at his conception and will whirl on to other things at his death. It is a very large process. The more he finds his identity in it, the less energy he will invest in defending, adorning, and deluding himself about his physical existence, and the more his security will come to be grounded in such immensity that he can, without terror, acknowledge fully the fictional nature of his ego identity. But this is a long way down the road.

Mature planning will incorporate the cycle referred to in Chapter VII: equilibrium to tension-seeking to goal-striving to attainment and equilibrium. We are born into a world of cycles—diurnal rotation of the earth bringing day and night, revolution of the planet around the sun giving the seasons, the moon's circling causing tides. Long-range plans of any kind will acknowledge that rest is needed daily, that offices are not manned on weekends, that tensions can be periodically tethered and resumed, and that a pace can be found and adopted suitable to maximum efficiency and happiness. Some people need eight hours' sleep, others less. Some people (not necessarily less mature) require more leisure and vacation time than others. Mature planning for the future embodies as part of its success potential the kind of efficiency that takes into account physical and mental limitations and paces accordingly, reduces the corrosive effects of frustration, and provides for the possibility of failure.

The mature person does plan, and plans do bring frustration. But since the mature person tolerates frustration easily enough to retain self-control and avoid excessive strain and anxiety, there is no incompatibility between planning for the future and maturing.

[7]

As we have remarked, love must start with love of self; anyone who does not love himself cannot love anyone else. Loving oneself must begin with self-respect. And this has to do with first accepting oneself.

How do you "accept" yourself? This is like possessing yourself. If you do any of these things—love, or accept, or possess your own self, it is implied that some *thing* has to do the loving or accepting or possessing. What is that? If you accept yourself, what does the accepting? You can accept your raincoat. But when you accept *you*, there must be something underlying the idea of self deeper than the self accepted.

This is related closely to the philosophic dilemma of the mind understanding itself. As long as there is part of the mind stepping outside to "understand" the rest of it, then that part will not be understood until a still further portion goes farther outside to understand *it*, and so on indefinitely.

"Accepting oneself" necessarily involves this infinite series of steps. It is precisely this infinite series that does the accepting, that does the understanding and loving. But the self *is* accepted, the mind is understood. If a given individual wears his blinders, then he is unaware of the acceptance of himself. He is simply *unaware* that he loves himself. He is unaware of this reality because he deliberately keeps himself from being aware. He has limited his awareness for reasons of comfort. He cuts himself off from this reality at the request of his ego, which is not concerned with infinite series, but with promoting its own limited importance and grooming its outlandish image. As long as he keeps himself unaware that he loves himself, he will be unable to love anyone else. He may go through some counterfeit motions—some of the rituals of love to combat loneliness, to elicit reciprocal affection for ego nourishment, or to satisfy a sense of drama—but he will be cut off from loving. He may even feel romantic attachments called into play by sexual needs, but he will not love.

*The capacity to love is directly related to a degree of awareness of reality.*

Much that passes for love in fiction, tradition, and social concepts has nothing to do with love. Jealousy, possessiveness, sexual hunger, sadistic control, conditional affection ("I will love you *if*—"), neurotic dependency—none of these is love or a component of love.

The mature person loves beyond need.

An old French proverb reads, "To love is to be weak. To be loved is to be strong." This speaks of paired relationships in which the one who cares more is more vulnerable. The one who cares less can work the other to his advantage. As long as power of this kind is considered the desirable end of a relationship, the saying is true. Since it implies this, it says in effect, "Be careful not to love, lest you become vulnerable."

This kind of invulnerability is guaranteed to lock one out of further growth. The ego is vulnerable anyway, and there is more than a hint of tragedy in spending life's energies in a way that tends to prevent awakening to the greater invulnerability of finding out who you are and being able to love. "Being loved" has its gratifications, but to set about loving in order to be loved in return is futile. The nature of love does not allow it to be employed as a means to any end. As soon as it is recruited to some other service, it ceases to be love. Loving is an outward act, an end in itself. You don't pursue and capture it. One can't "have love" for someone or something. "Love isn't love till you give it away." The outward quality of love illustrates its kinship to the same infinite series of processes that characterizes understanding. It might be noted that volition has the same property: Einstein commented on this in a discussion of freedom and determinism. "I will to light my pipe. But what is behind the will? Volition." And something not named is behind the volition. And if we label that something, there will be something behind that, and so on. When we realize that there is no end to such a process, it dawns on us that anything we enclose in a concept and label with a name is stamped with limitation. Love removes itself step by step from the confinement of identity with either a label or any individual ego. It has a powerful effect on the ego, and a love object can be an apparent condensation point—a focus of feeling, a bridge from one ego to the other, more direct than any other kind of communication. But when it or its designated objects are grasped—conceived as possessions—love withdraws a step. It will not be confined. When it is pursued, the act of pursuit causes it to recede again.

But if it is true that the capacity to love is directly related to a degree of awareness of reality, how can pursuing love cause it to recede? The answer is that awareness is not possession. It is not pursuit. The aware person is one who has quit trying to see the stars by building more signal fires. The mature person understands and loves; he doesn't pursue or possess.

[8]

It is difficult to understand the connection between loving one other person and loving one's fellow man.

When a love object is sensed as the focal point of romantic or obsessive feeling, this often entails specific exclusion of anyone else; this is part of the "nature" of love, it seems.

I believe we have to be very suspicious of this exclusivity factor. When desire and romantic feelings condense on one person, it is certainly "natural," because nature, at least in heterosexual relationships, fixed it so there will be maximum likelihood that reproduction results from the liaison. A man and woman's staying together is more likely when romantic feelings are added to mere sexual hunger (always more transitory), and staying together over a period of time maximizes chances of impregnation. Nature utilizes and shapes the elements of love for the purpose of perpetuating life. There is nothing wrong and certainly nothing "unnatural" in the process, or in enjoying it when it comes to us, but it would be a mistake to imagine that this is the totality of love. The popular belief concerning the relationship between romantic love and generic love seems to be that the wider caring for all of humanity is a transformation—perhaps a perversion—of the more "natural" drive to love one person. The reverse is true: Love is limitless, and although a portion of it can be grabbed and used by biological urge to illuminate and ennoble a fundamentally sexual relationship (and this is nice—love ennobles anything it touches), it is a mistake to think that this is all there is to love. It is a mistake that enslaves, because it leaves that part of love in the control of hungers that can be sated, and that once sated tend to drop the feelings as no longer needed.

The mature person does not love out of need. Realization that romantic or obsessive love is only a specially utilized and arbitrarily shaped aspect of love frees a person to enjoy it thoroughly, but to transform it, after sexual fires are banked, into its wider context, which is independent of physical processes. A maturing person, drawing on this wider context of love, finds himself the master of his loving and not the slave. And he will find that he tends to be more the master of his passions. He can and probably will continue to love the one person as he did, but will not sense the flavors of exclusivity. He will escape jealousy, possessiveness, and dependency, which are not part of love anyway. Whether he remains "true" to an original love is important only in that loving tends to avoid hurting someone loved; and being the master of his passions, the mature person will not need to indulge in actions that would be harmful to a loved partner, assuming the partner has a reasonable degree of maturity and is not neurotically or irrationally demanding. When both partners share a high degree of maturity, fidelity, in the Victorian sense, is not a slavish goal, and successful possessiveness will not be a factor in binding them together. Staying together will cease to be necessary to a sense of security, and the bond will be a mutual desire for each other's company rather than a sense of need or duty. Partnership love is complicated, but it does not have to be pain-ridden or anxiety-fraught.

Above all, a full realization of the true nature of romantic love (even when flavored with obsession) as a special, useful, and limited aspect of something wider and more powerful, gives those who really love, the possibility of retaining some control without stifling the feelings.

Wider love—generic love—is not merely a transformation or perversion of romantic love.

Although there can be sublimation of sex drives into non-genital channels, and although this thwarts a natural purpose (and is unusual), it is neither "unnatural" nor necessary to maturing. Sexual excursion as a source of pleasure cannot be condemned as dangerous in an era of adequate intellect. The means are at hand for the control of disease and unwanted pregnancy.

The ascetic notion of the necessity of suppressing sexual desire probably stemmed from the almost inevitable turmoil that arose from sexual indulgence in times past (and alas, present)—turmoil not conducive to spiritual growth. Jealous rivals, anxieties of abandonment, unwanted children, venereal disorders, social ostracism, and legal strife all stand in the way of emotional progress for a pilgrim on the path of maturity, and the ascetic reaction was one of shunning in horror all carnal relations. This reactive recoiling from something clearly in our nature is itself unnatural. It is as arrestive of emotional progress as the opposite practice of uncontrolled indulgence, which is a symptom, not a cause, of emotional immaturity.

## CHAPTER XII

## *Human Nature?*

### [1]

The ancients felt that man had to rise above his nature. Modern maturing individuals feel that it is *within* the nature of man to progress to maturity. Intellect has provided the means to progress in this way, avoiding both the extremes of asceticism and compulsive sensual indulgence.

The connection, then, between romantic loving and the wider caring that we call love of fellow man is that the former is really part of the latter. Both are natural. Both are to be enjoyed fully; neither need enslave. You cannot really love an individual without at least sensing that greater love of which it is a part. Anyone who has been in love, really in love, with another human being has felt at moments that he loves the whole world—which includes himself and every living thing in it.

We have seen how nature utilized competition for the selection of excellence among diversely developed life forms, and how that process, having culminated in man, gave rise to a new and unique situation on the planet—one in which competition is counterindicated. Competition among diverging types is not only no longer needed, it is poisonous. It must now be replaced by cooperation.

If religion as we have known it has anything to offer man, it is the idea of cooperation through caring that runs through all doctrine, quietly, stubbornly insisting that man will save himself individually and collectively only in this way.

In the necessary transition from competition to cooperation, the question arises: Is it in man's nature to continue to compete, to hate, to struggle, since he evolved from a world in which he would simply have perished without competitive instincts? And is it normal and natural for him to leave undeveloped the capacity for love and affirmation of life that he apparently possesses? Or is the failure to cultivate this potential evidence of illness? Man cannot even put to effective use the rational part of his mind while these instincts stand in the way.

Psychiatrist G. B. Chisholm, writing in the *Survey Graphic* in 1947, says, "The difficulty man has with himself is that he cannot use his highly developed intellect effectively because of his neurotic fears, his prejudices, his fanaticisms, his unreasoning hates, his equally unreasoning devotions; in fact, his failure to reach emotional maturity, or mental health." Here is a psychiatric view that failure to reach the potential is illness.

It is significant that the major religions of the world have a common tenet: It is necessary to love. It is further significant that this unifying idea is the only aspect of religion that survives and transcends dogma and the uses of religious forms for temporal power—for the control of masses through fear and superstition. The Spanish Inquisition was short-lived. The concept of love persists.

Now, under the pressure of the dangers posed by man's enormously powerful weapons capability, the need is present and strong to develop a different kind of human—to mass-produce this kind, so to speak—a human able to grow up and leave behind the destructive instincts he has trailed from an evolutionary past, and develop fully the cooperative faculties that appear to be present in some embryonic form in his psyche.

"In order that the human race may survive on this planet, it is necessary that there should be enough people in enough places in the world who do not have to fight each other, who are not the kinds of people who will fight each other, and who are the kinds of people who will take effective measures whenever it is necessary to prevent other people's fighting," says Chisholm. Overstreet echoes this: "Smiting each other on the cheek, and smiting back, actually does not work—however highly an immature world may rate it, as 'common sense.' It is common nonsense. Therefore 'a new commandment I give unto you'—to develop enough emotional maturity to take the initiative in breaking the vicious circle of smiting and being smitten. This is the commandment—laid upon man by his own social nature—that has, more than any other, been given lip-service and then disobeyed in action. It has been disobeyed because those who have given it lip-service have too often been too immature to act it out or even to understand its deeper implications. They have thought that it required them to deny their own nature, or, by some divine grace, to transcend that nature; they have not realized that what it asked was a mature fulfillment of that nature." H. A. Overstreet, *The Mature Mind* (New York: W. W. Norton & Co., 1949), p. 104.

Again the idea that it is not only necessary but *natural* to outgrow the hostilities we inherit, and it is evidence of illness to fail to outgrow them.

It is not unreasonable to assume that if maturing is within our nature, and not something to be developed and tacked onto our nature, then techniques for achieving some level of maturity should be available from within, and it is more a matter of discovering than developing them. I think this is true.

[2]

To what do we look then for a starting point?

First off, it may be wrong to imagine that at any time in life we are in need of a special starting point from which to move toward maturing. Very few of us are actually deteriorating in this regard. Even fewer could be considered on dead center. Most of us are maturing anyway, although perhaps not at a rate that our potential would allow if inhibiting factors weren't at work. The real question ought to be, "What action can we take to bring up to full power the process of maturing?"

And here there may be no frontal assault possible. The oblique approach is more clearly indicated. It may be more a matter of stepping back—relaxing—to let something already within our nature operate unhindered. Trying to force yourself to sleep is not a cure for insomnia.

How do you stand back, out of the way of some process you are asked to assume exists? First, by taking the position that you have nothing to lose. Gestures of this kind are not leaps into the dark. There is no irreversible mistake possible in this suggested first step.

Specifically there is no advantage to be gained in efforts spent trying to "be mature," or to "become more mature," and I doubt that many people would be so motivated anyway. Instead, the indicated efforts would be toward different goals.

Do you feel that you are trapped into habits and reactions you'd like to be free of? Then you are motivated to start freeing yourself of enslaving habits. Make this a goal. If it is habitual, when a member of the family makes a mistake, for all the others to jump on him angrily or to make fun of him, do the opposite at the next opportunity. It might surprise everybody, including you, the first time.

One way to get out of a rut is to develop (deliberately, this time) a tolerance for mild discomfort. This is not asceticism. Asceticism is a taste for heavier discomfort, and as an end in itself it is a perversion—a vicious form of pride. But the development of a tolerance for mild discomfort is useful in areas where the discomfort has some value. In areas where the discomfort is deep and neurotically rooted, it will not be advisable to try, because the failure might cause further retreat, and such areas (for example, pathological shyness and anxiety on asserting oneself) are matters for therapy. But there are areas where prodding oneself can immediately bring results. A minor but parallel example might be getting into a swimming pool where you dread the shock of the water temperature, but where you know once in you will enjoy swimming. Jarring yourself out of tiny ruts like this can set patterns that will eventually enable you to handle bigger ones.

If you feel that fate dictates too much of your daily condition and actions, seize the role of fate every now and then, even if a sudden decision brings a less desirable outcome of some issue. The important thing is your having had a hand in it. A sudden decision can still follow a modicum of thought about the situation. The thing to be avoided is thinking in circles and delaying any decision at all until fate has decided for you.

[3]

When certain problems have resulted in this thinking in circles, worrying over the same path time and again, one "decision" might be simply to walk away from them. Go to other problems, or take a nap. It is surprising how often solutions come from relaxing the mind, turning down the effort.

It is possible to make a goal of getting outside yourself by *really* thinking about someone else's problem for a time. Attention directed away from the self for a period does three things: (1) it puts your own problems into a somewhat better perspective; (2) it develops empathy; (3) it begins to make you think of your own self as a means to an end.

Perspective gives a base for values that make many of your personal problems seem as small as they really are. Did you ever visit someone's home and find out later that your hosts had been upset because new slip-covers or draperies due before you arrived had not been delivered? You didn't know the draperies or slip-covers were old, or wrong, or whatever it was about them that caused distress, and you could see how meaningless the concern was. Had the new ones been in place, it would have made absolutely no difference in your visit. In broadcasting I have sometimes had to leave out for lack of time material I wanted to include, and have felt bad about it. But the viewer knows only what is broadcast. What is left out doesn't exist. We waste much energy on concerns like this; getting away from ourselves helps to avoid this sort of unnecessary negative feeling.

The development of empathy is resoundingly its own reward. It expands your base. It is a source of some of the richest feelings in human experience, and in the long run it contributes to the kind of human community in which maturing of other individuals is facilitated.

Seeing yourself as a means to an end is a gateway to unlimited growth. You can't avoid being your own center. Self-centeredness is not in itself a bad thing. But if you are nothing but a hub, you are severely limited. If, on the other hand, you are an expanding wheel of which the hub (your ego) is only a part (and a part concerned with serving the spokes and rim), you have set yourself in a world where you can transcend the limitations of ego.

One cannot stress too strongly the tangible and immediate results that can come from very small moves toward getting outside yourself. Even a single honest effort to become concerned with the problem of someone else brings reward. Mostly we simply do not try, because it seems there is nothing in it for us. In theory, there *is* nothing in it. As a practice, it can be astonishingly rewarding.

Both the positive step of an effort to become concerned with another's problem and the more passive ploy of turning away from one's own problems momentarily represent moves to break a compulsive, repetitive pattern that has proved ineffective. Attempting to develop some tolerance for mild discomfort likewise tends to take one out of the merely reactive rut of dealing "characteristically" with each of life's moments. The efforts have the effect of enhancing self-actualization. They are creative acts.

These humble (and, indeed, cliché) suggestions are important because they can be followed by nearly everyone, and because they are less likely to fail than nobler, larger schemes embarked on prematurely. Further, they have the effect of demonstrating our ability to set foot on a road to maturing; they prove the ideas we dream about but believe beyond an "ordinary person."

A number of bigger steps are available to those who become seekers. Creative psychology, Zen and Yoga disciplines, psycho-analysis, systems such as Gurdjieff's and Ouspensky's, all strive to teach the individual something about himself and liberate him from the bondage of reactive living, to awaken creativity and self-activation.

There is a danger of getting "hung up" on a system or teacher—it is evidence that the maturing process has stopped. They are meant to be only means to an end. Building a tolerance for discomfort, for example, is a useful technique. Relied on steadily, it becomes asceticism. Carried too far, it becomes masochism.

Think of the phrase "everything in moderation" as meaning on a deeper level "everything as a means." Every *thing* as a means. When a technique or discipline ceases to be a means, a tool, it becomes first a crutch, and in time tends to permanent disability. And then it becomes a pen, an institutional structure with rising and thickening walls. It imprisons.

# CHAPTER XIII

## A *Kind of Immortality*

### [1]

Earlier I mentioned thinking of *oneself* as a means rather than an end. The ego self is useful as an early means to security. The function of ego is to help an organism preserve its integrity, to help it endure. When this integrity is threatened, the self-preservation instinct in the organism is inflamed and thrown on alert until the danger is passed. To be effective, an instinct of self-preservation requires a high degree of coordination of the organs of sense and action. The chain—information-evaluation-decision-implementation—must be well integrated and economical of time. The input (information) at the sense-organ end, the evaluation and decision steps in the brain, and the implementation of decisions by muscle groups must all take place in split seconds. The consciousness that comes from partial knowledge and the necessity for efficient and largely correct decisions for survival and security are the stimulus-complex that give rise to ego. Ego is the confederation of these faculties and processes. In any case wherein the level of maturity is such that security requires organic survival as the highest-priority goal, ego tends to dominate consciousness.

The human organism, however, has resources of security that

transcend physical survival. Because of this, ego individuality can be controlled and recruited to higher causes, one of which is establishing a concept of self as a means rather than as a thing—a means to outward action and concern. This puts ego in a limiting perspective and permits limitless growth. If a person fails to achieve a concept of himself as means, he will gain no degree of autonomy, but remain a puppet, reacting characteristically to every stimulus of his environment.

As we examined earlier, there appear to be a number of levels of awareness of human potential for maturing. Beneath the lowest level is a state of no awareness whatever. The condition is noteworthy because it exists in a very large group of people. These people sense that life could be better, but view its shortcomings as belonging to the world. They are what they are, but circumstances have conspired against them. It does not occur to them that they could be improved, or that improvement in themselves might improve what they regard as the world. Up through the levels discussed in the early pages of Chapter II, we arrive at what sages have called a condition of enlightenment.

At the highest discernible level (one can't say: "Finally, at the top"—there may be no top), there are a very few humans spread out through history, possibly some of them alive now, who are free of any frustration, suffering, limitation of consciousness, or bondage to time or space. They see what we call reality as illusion, they depend on nobody and nothing outside themselves, they enjoy an ongoing ecstasy of some sort that enables them to "give up" sensual pleasures without any sense of self-denial (much as a successful adult would "give up" riding a tricycle). Apparently these truly liberated souls even cheat death through the realization that it is as illusory as physical existence. W. Y. Evans-Wentz wrote, "No master of yoga ever dies in the normal manner, unless, perchance, he be killed suddenly and unexpectedly; he merely relinquishes the physical form which he has come to recognize as no more than a garment to be put on or off as desired, in full consciousness while immersed in the ecstatic condition of mind wherein the Clear Light ever shines. . . . The Great *Yogin* transcends normal processes by voluntarily relinquishing his old, out-worn body and taking a new body, without suffering any break in the continuity of his consciousness."*

Two classes of people can readily believe this: the very gullible and the master yogis. In between these classes are those of us who may find our credulity stretched rather badly, but who at least have the ability to suspend judgment. Sensible people of a century ago would have regarded a description of a jetliner or a television set as overdrawn and unlikely ever to come into being, but the really wise would not have shut out the possibilities. This is about all we can do with respect to this level. If these marvels exist as described, the road to them is undoubtedly long and arduous. Setting shorter range goals and moving a step at a time are recommended. But a direction is needed.

Yoga discipline appears to be a way. Christianity proclaims itself to be the way. Tao, the great Chinese system of enlightenment, is named by a word meaning "way." Buddhism is a Way, listing a Noble Eightfold Path.

There may be other paths and "ways," even in Western civilization (which has not generally encouraged exploration in these matters, even contorting its nominal faith, Christianity, into a creed that blessed and furthered competitive materialism and a horrendous idea of original sin).

Still, the general inability of an immature society to recognize mature people leads us to suspect that such people may move among us in greater numbers than might be thought. They did not all have gurus. If they had converted to any formal religion they would likely have outgrown the ritualistic and dogmatic aspects of it early. Some of these mature people may have come up through no "way" but their own. If they exist even in greater numbers than might be thought, they are still probably a tiny minority. And they are not publicized. Certainly they are not seeking publicity, since doing so would be evidence of not being what they actually are.

* *Tibetan Yoga and Secret Doctrine* (London: Oxford University Press, 1935).

But it is likely that they see themselves as means to some end
transcending preservation of ego.

[2]

Let's deal for a moment with a gnawing doubt, a doubt that
says: How certain can we be that any effort of any kind can increase the percentage of people who mature? Might it not be a
fixed statistical sprinkling among masses, and of a nature that no
amount of education or cultural security or psychological technique can increase?

To my knowledge there is no authoritative proof that this might
not be the case. A society could conceivably be highly and widely
educated without any increase in the proportion of citizens enlightened with the insights that attend and characterize maturity.

Without such proof I can only advance a reason for behaving
*as though increasing maturing were possible.*

We are using as axioms the assumptions that human life has
a meaning of some sort, or that it can find or create one; that
it is desirable that human life continue (not necessarily unchanged); and that there is such a thing as relative maturity,
however imprecisely defined. I have further added as informal
hypotheses that human societies requiring and contributing to
maturity of their citizens are structurable and have already, on a
relative scale, been brought into being; that the more mature
citizen and such citizens in greater numbers will, through their
societies, direct human knowledge to greater human good; and
finally, that this greater human good will be found in identification with, and working for, evolution. By this is not meant
Darwinian evolution, but the broader process of which natural
selection is a part—the evolution that leads itself through the
steps from blind chance to competitive force to cooperating
mind, increasing complexity of organization and levels of consciousness at each of several stages.

If the percentage of people who can mature in the sense we

are talking about *is* in a fixed ratio, and if that ratio is impervious to the pressure of any human institution or technique (in the way that decay of radioactive elements is fixed and impervious to temperature, pressure, etc.), the breakthrough may come from some unexpected quarter. It may come simply from the environment created by a saturation of information, whether or not the information is formally educational in nature.

And, of course, it may not come at all.

But in the absence of proof, further search for proof often remains unproductive, whereas proceeding as though proof were in hand often produces results. In formal religions this is called faith. The term has been badly abused by applied religions, but its validity is demonstrable.

The reason—the justification—for operating as though maturing on a wide human scale is possible through human effort, is that if such efforts succeed, there will be immense reward; and if they fail, we will be no worse off than we are now. The satisfactions will lie in the establishment and reinforcement of purpose so badly needed now by mankind; the deconstricting of the channels to personal maturity (often clogged by a society's demand for conformity and allegiance); the awakening of man to the compatibility of personal interest and social good; the reduction and eventual elimination of the waste and agony of emotional darkness—the hatreds, fears, wars, civil strife, the squandering of life, the continuing demand of Moloch for youngsters to destroy, even in twentieth-century urban America.

At the moment the rallying point for maturing may not be so much a conscious feeling of the need to mature, as an overwhelming sense of the wrong of wasting human resources (even more than the danger of exterminating all humanity). "There must be a better way!" is the cry.

Further, I deeply believe that there is born in every human a potential for maturing. It seems inconceivable that this potential would be installed and then be hermetically sealed against realization. Whether or not we have at present the skills to allow and help everyone to mature, the possibility remains with everyone born, and nature does not endow life forms with characteristics that are not capable of fruition under certain circumstances.

In light of the past behavior of evolution, there is every indication that something will unlock the human urge to move ahead as the spearpoint of life. The happiest individuals born in the next generations will be those who feel they are contributing to this effort.

[3]

How would large numbers of highly mature people relate to each other, and what kind of society would they form? When we examine these questions we are talking about the future—a possible future. Such a future is one of those things "not inevitable—only necessary."

We can assume that more mature people would be better able than less mature ones to agree on aims and goals, to plan for a future desirable and possible, and to carry forward those plans with a minimum of wasted effort.

But at the present moment there is little agreement not only on how to achieve future goals but on what those goals ought to be. The sickness of the twentieth century could be that we have not formed or found a sense of purpose commensurate with the liberating effects of political freedom and leisure-producing physical power our age ushered in. The Communist world has come closer than anything in our time to a unifying concept of human destiny, but its failure lies in the fact that it can appeal only to masses who are extremely oppressed; and as soon as it administers promised relief, it must impose its own repression in an attempt to survive, because everything it delivers appears to be at the cost of hope. As a result it is transformed by decay more rapidly than other forms of government. Communist theory appeared in part as a reaction against the mischief Christian doctrine had brought on mankind. This doctrine had nothing to do with the teachings of Christ but rather with the propensity of organized priestcraft to countenance wealth and privilege for a few, and with the related idea of original sin, firmly installed in the Church by St. Augustine four centuries after Jesus lived, destroying self-respect as a heritage in order to enhance respect for and obedience to a religious institution. Reactions against this sort of thinking have ranged from Puritanism to communism, and each has fallen into the same trap—the substitution of one set of dogma for another, each finally asserting an authority against which self-respect is intolerable.

No matter what system rises against totalitarian suppression of self-respect, it will be doomed to *become* totalitarian suppression of self-respect until humanity has crossed some threshold of maturity as yet unattained—a threshold beyond which there will be no need for the kinds of authority we constantly invite.

The struggle against each new tyranny is inevitably regarded by those governing as perverse. It is thought to be something in human nature. The term "human nature" is usually employed in this negative sense—something to be fought down, overcome, risen above. The tragic irony of our being ashamed of what is really our very best nature is rooted in the idea of original sin.

"The 'will to disobedience' . . . found in all of us now appears to be merely the expression of the inevitable conflict between a helpless creature trying to grow into its proper independence and an environment that the child, in his immaturity, can neither understand nor master. . . .

"At a time when the maturity concept had not yet even begun to exert its clarifying influence, it is not surprising that man thus misjudged man. Pelagius was, it would appear, more nearly right than Augustine; but an age that was still in psychological darkness was prepared to accept the easier, because more obvious, view of man's inherent will to evil, rather than the more difficult view of man's inherent power to grow into goodness."† (A more potent reason than the obviousness for formulating the doctrine of original sin was that it permitted a going organization to

† H. A. Overstreet, *The Mature Mind*.

exert temporal power by setting up a universal defect in all humanity and then dispensing remedy at the price of obedience.)

And so we thrash about in our search for purpose. We feel religion has let us down, political philosophers have let us down, material success is empty, corrosive of morale, and cynicism creeps on us like a blight. The paralysis of will we all sense must be due, at least partly, to the question whispering deep inside us, "Will to what?"

If we are at last tumbling to the idea that exercising that will for growth in power and numbers—felling more trees, mining more metal, making more automobiles, damming more rivers, building more weapons—is a certain road to disaster, then we begin to understand paralysis of will.

If we feel that we must abandon progress, on which our entire evolutionary history has been based, we can understand the cynicism that must be born of a sense of tragedy and doom. Even our higher qualities, those that motivate us to efforts in the alleviation of suffering and the feeding of the starving, show us the folly of making it possible for more humans to produce still more humans, who will eventually face these problems of starvation and poison in greater numbers than now.

H. G. Wells said in A *Modern Utopia*, "Will is stronger than fact; it can mold and overcome fact. But this world has still to discover its Will."

[4]

The search for an ultimate goal might be futile. This doesn't mean, though, that the search for an aim and a purpose is futile.

The thesis of this book, again, is that continuing to mature is possible, that it must be facilitated, and that a sound short-range aim for humanity is a coordination of efforts to that end. Long-range aims and goals can be left to more mature humans and human societies. It is probable that more mature humans will build more mature societies and that more mature societies in turn will encourage the further maturing of individuals.

This circle can be entered. Although it is possible that it can be entered at the collective level, there is historic evidence that it is more likely to be entered at the individual level. Great ideas contributed by great men are, it is true, often absorbed and perverted by the world, but the great men and the great ideas keep coming along, and each leaves some irreducible residue through which the world is better than it was before. Mature people tend to transform society. There have probably been too few mature societies to judge whether they transform humans in any significant numbers, and this is why I believe it may be more important to concentrate on the means of enabling individuals to mature. At any rate, while a mature human can exist in a woefully immature society, a really mature society could not be made up of very immature citizens.

To come back to our speculation on the kind of society a large group of citizens of considerable maturity might build:

This would be, I believe, a society with no foundation on a status quo, however exalted. At a certain point a society, to endure, would have to abandon absolutes of morality and eternal verity, and organize itself around processes of change and a relativistic concept of our presently polarized ideas of freedom and bondage, good and evil, etc. One man's good is another man's evil. An ignorant man's bondage might be a philosopher's freedom. If we are to have human independence and the dignity of individual tastes and liberties, we cannot impose general definitions of right and wrong.

The centeredness of such a society would still be precise. It would not be anarchic. (The center of the earth is precise, and while the axis of up and down is not the same for the Londoner as it is for the citizen of Buenos Aires, in each case it passes through the center of the earth.) This is less ambiguous than a universal and parallel (intrinsic) concept of up and down, which leads nowhere.

The center of the society we're envisioning here would be the worth and meaning of the individual human, and the idea of his place and responsibility in all of evolution—his significance as life.

We almost made it once in history. The United States of America was founded on the idea of individual rights and dignity (Greek democracy did not quite grasp this, and in any case, it did not extend it to everyone) and would have become a fulfillment at least of the European Dream if it hadn't been for a succession of reversals. It declared all men to be created equal and then it upheld slavery. It proclaimed individualism and then embraced nationalism. It put civilian life first and then institutionalized the military.

Although the United States has been an improvement over anything before it, the time for its idea has not come and will not come until a higher percentage of people achieve sufficient maturity to see and seize on the direction of destiny—the concept of a task. At that point comfort will not erode morale. Success will not spoil. The sense of urgency about the task will not depend on the stimulation of external circumstance—threats and repugnances—but will be self-generated and related more to an attraction.

The task is the furtherance of evolution now already in the hands of man.

What is this immense stewardship of the universe vested in us? And are we the only form of life anywhere at this level? We have come up alone from the interior of the world (that is, from the "interiorized" aspect of matter). If other intelligent beings exist anywhere among all those billions of billions of stars, we have no sign of their presence. But we are here, and for the first time, life dares think about all the rest of the road. Man "is . . . the only living being for whom the stimulating impulse without which there can be no action is not confined to the perception of an immediate end, but comes from a *confrontation with the whole of the future.*"‡

‡ Teilhard de Chardin, *Activation of Energy*, trans. 1969 (New York: Harcourt Brace Jovanovich, 1970), p. 391.

We have been called from play and from dreaming.

For all the pressure of immediate problems and the diversions they create, we have been prodded awake and informed of our place in the cosmic thrust of life, and anything less than the responsibility this entails leaves our existence meaningless. We are to be the spearpoint of the world's drive to live.

The task is one to make all previous human endeavor seem small. Our animal survival instincts, our competitive drive, coupled with our newfound intellect, have given us dominance and propelled us out onto a new field. We are in a transitional stage. It has been observed that present-day humanity is the "missing link." Professor John Platt calls us the Step to Man. Teilhard de Chardin believes we are just now crossing the threshold to an awakening that will carry life on toward what he calls the Omega Point. Evolution, up to now diverging, spreading outward through a variety of species, has picked one that will guide it from here on in a convergence toward a goal that represents full realization of the "within" or immanence of matter, full self-determination, and a maximum (maximizing) state of complexity in the universal energy total.

Whether man is that pivotal being cannot be determined from the vantage point we occupy at the moment. Certainly man is unique in this planet's vital history. But so was the self-replicating molecule and the cell and the central nervous system. However unique in essence, man may be simply another plateau from which life will build to still higher plateaus. In either case there is a role to be played, and for the first time a "plateau" of nature, because it has choices and intellect, has responsibility.

# CHAPTER XIV

## The Future and the Potential

### [1]

One of the fears we have in this time of danger from environmental degradation is that even if we reverse certain trends and save ourselves from a pollution death, it will be at the cost of progress.

Our happiness as a species has had its roots in growth. Expansion has been an important part of success. We took seriously the biblical injunction to "be fruitful and multiply." In every way, we have grown, but we live on a finite surface—on a planet of limited resources. How can we now continue to progress if we are running out of space and materials? Obviously we can't, if progress is defined as we have defined it in the past. But we can redefine progress.

First we must limit our numbers—level off the population at some manageable quantity and set some ceiling on the amount of energy to be used by each person. (It need not be exactly the same amount of energy for everyone; some people will have more call for energy than others, but if its distribution is to be uneven, then the percentages must be of some agreed total per unit time.) Then we can turn our efforts to progressing in some new ways that will not tax the planet and could increase the quality of life.

Such a future society will first of all have gotten control of its population levels and instituted the practices of conserving resources and recycling wastes. Then it will form its concept of progress around the increase of justice, the improvement of education, the eradication of poverty and disease, the exploration of the psyche, the strengthening of a sense of purpose, the concerted moving forward of the task. It will have abandoned the simplistic (and often erroneous) idea that "more is better"; it will have begun to produce an ever-greater percentage of people who will have outgrown status seeking, addictive and compulsive tendencies, superstition and overdependency and all the culturally nurtured neuroses that perpetuate themselves in immature, traditionbound societies; it will, in fact, have established "traditions" which, instead of stemming from past habit, will be oriented toward a "willed future." This will be possible only through a fundamental sense of allegiance to life. Harvey Wheeler says, "Ultimately, institutions follow allegiances."

This is not a utopia. It is simply an improved culture.

Such a society will have faced the choices in population control—massive destruction by weapons, widespread famine, unchecked disease, birth control on a world scale.

This society will be concerned about the total quantity of nonreplaceable raw materials on earth and will set its levels of consumer use at a pace that will allow a good possibility of the development of substitutes, and eventual mining of the moon and other planets. It will also have brought recycling processes to an efficient level, so that the nonrecovery factor will be small.

The maintenance and increase of technical sophistication will be much a part of such a future society. The community will simply have gotten away from the idea "if it can be done it must be done." There will be much more intelligent selection of what "must be done."

Could our society survive among other societies not so enlightened—societies that would not hesitate to overwhelm it by force? In these circumstances it might maintain a force of arms, and although it might not be able at all times to avoid war, it will be able to avoid the kinds of action that would contribute to an atmosphere of war, and to the inward destruction of its moral life: overkill in defensive arming, a stance of arrogant superiority and necessary dominance, failure to take into account the human factors in engagements. It will not export ideology, and it will probably not put survival ahead of moral integrity. If forced to a choice of death as a nation or the surrender of its moral values in the pursuit of combat, it might perish in the belief that its type would appear again on earth. It will refuse to give nationalism the highest priority. In doing so it will be acting (for the first time in history) as individuals have acted at times—realizing the mortality inherent in organization, and identifying with an ideal higher than its own survival.

The world has already progressed to a point where human allegiance can be seen to belong to humanity. Nations will be with us for a long time, and the concept of nationhood is useful in organizing social action. Some nations are worth defending because some nations are better than others, but no nation is worth the final allegiance of a human being. And not even a "good" nation is worth preserving at the total cost of the ideals that have made it good.

Nationalism as a means is tolerable; as an end it is vicious. It gravitates toward imperialism. While the world is getting used to the idea that imperialism is simply no longer tenable, the need for more citizen enlightenment on this is pronounced. Greed is a potent and vital trait.

"While economists carry on learned debates about whether any nation's empire has been a source of profit, there is no disputing the fact that firms and individuals have reaped huge profits from imperialism. The West has yet to appreciate the full implications of the fact that it is no longer possible to do this. However, the future of democracy in the world may depend on the fact that the new nations are beginning their efforts at development under the new conditions which prevent imperialist exploitation. The logic of the world situation runs counter to imperialism. The ideologies of the new nations are anti-imperialistic. This combination may force the new nations to learn a lesson that no civilization has ever learned before: how to institute the principles of democracy in the world community as well as domestically." *Britannica Perspectives*, Vol. II, p. 478.

The mature society, if it comes about, will most likely take the form of a world community, partly because mass communication is inexorably building the shared knowledge, the economic ties, the sense of a common future that will incline the world to unity. The way is being prepared for some sort of world civilization. Whether or not it is "mature," whether it is even tolerable, will depend in great measure on the universality of education. If education remains specialized and structured for the few, tending thus to breed experts in isolated disciplines, particularly in the field of government, then there will be too many laymen—there will be gaps between the man in the tower and the man in the street. Worst of all, there will be a gap between the governing and the governed that will blight any chances of democracy.

It is doubtful that education can be kept from anyone in the world for very long: Information flow is a flood. Television will soon be showered everywhere on the globe like cosmic radiation —cheap sets in the Australian outback will carry the same material seen in northern Canada and Easter Island and suburban London and Hokkaido. This material will not necessarily be classifiable as academic education, but it will be educational nonetheless, and the main thing it will do (it is doing so now) will be to create a world atmosphere that finds intolerable the denial of opportunity to any human being anywhere.

Education came in with mammals, the young learning from parents, and if nature's use of education to date can be extrapolated, we can assume that this field in some applied form is likely to be a key factor in increasing the percentage of humans who reach sufficient maturity to move life forward out of its present danger and toward a sensed fulfillment.

It is hardly imaginable that a mature society will fail to give education a very high priority. By "education" must be understood the effort to lead to understanding, not attempts to condition to citizenship.

Such a society will not use education directly to effect social change. Robert M. Hutchins says, "Educational reforms are likely to be the result, rather than the cause, of the alteration of social perspectives." Education will contribute to social good, but it must do so indirectly—obliquely by creating an atmosphere in which improvement can flower, rather than addressing itself to specifics. As soon as an educational system operates in the interest of a state or a goal such as industrialization or the success of an ideology or the verity of a religion or the promotion of a culture, it stands in danger of being counterproductive because it shifts subtly from education to conditioning.

[2]

If the best government is the least government, and if there will be more wisdom in a society of mature humans, then the government of such a society will be relatively nonapparent. Citizens will be obedient to the unenforceable. Rules of behavior will be simple and equitable, without emphasis on detailed legal language and enforcement procedures.

Religion in the mature society will be belief, perhaps a variety of beliefs, but in no case will it be organized for the control of masses nor around superstitions. Some sort of axis of destiny will be central to these faiths.

The society will be organized, as we said earlier, around processes of change. Some common will would be discernible, and I suspect that it will thrust in a line parallel to the religious aim.

Progress will no longer be regarded as merely technical and scientific progress. Refinements in these will continue, but they will be disciplined.

A decrease in anthropocentrism will enhance a sense of kinship with remaining life forms, which will be subject to humane regulation.

No human will want for education because of lack of financial resources.

Medicine and psychiatry will have less remedial emphasis and more purpose of prevention of disorder, although techniques of remedy will be improved.

Retribution as an element of justice will have vanished. The relationship of rights and responsibilities will be strengthened. Disputation will have changed in character (and diminished) with increased maturity, since much of emotional and self-defensive attitudes will be seen as unnecessarily clogging court proceedings. Courts will have streamlined their procedures to eliminate costly and time-consuming traditions.

The mature society will maintain police forces, most of whose work will be in areas of accident and disaster relief, and being on call for irreducible aberrant behavior. Police training will include not only rescue skills, restraint in the use of force, and sensitivity, but psychology and medicine; and their pay and their enjoyment of the respect of the community will be high.

The interface between computer work and human desires will be facilitated by cybernetic devices designed not so much with preprogrammed goals as with a high degree of random circuitry.

Leadership will make wide use of such cybernetic techniques. Leadership will long since have been recruited for other than father-figure or charismatic reasons. There will be in government more wisdom and less power-seeking.

Military forces designed to safeguard the sovereignty of state will reflect a new attitude of the states toward their sovereignty. The explosive game of supremacy will be controlled. This may seem impossible in light of the fact that a warlike nation can always force a peaceful one to defend itself or be overwhelmed, and only a superior force is deemed adequate to defense, but there is historic precedent for mutual advantage in avoiding armed conflict.

There is hardly a nation in existence today that is unaware

that it could not win a major war. If the world suffers another major war it will be because of some kind of mistake—some misassessment of another's motives, some error or inadequacy of communication. If statesmen can buy time, the possibility of such error or inadequacy can be reduced to a level of relative safety. And in the longer haul, there is always the possibility of more enlightenment in leadership.

Such a world will not be on a solid footing until individual maturing has progressed to a marked degree and its effects have seeped into social and political structures. Even then, war as we know it may not be eradicated, but transformed into some "moral equivalent," carrying with it all of the strife, but on less physically violent and self-destructive planes.

CHAPTER XV

## *"If You Meet the Buddha, Kill Him"*

The legend has it that a follower asked the guru where and how he could find the Buddha.

"If you meet the Buddha, kill him," was the guru's answer.

The apparently ambiguous response symbolized the necessity of recognizing who you really are, and implied an identification with a "universal" reality that transcends the dualism of subject-object thinking.

The Buddha, in other words, would be found within one, and at the desirable level of development one would not seek an external Buddha, but would have *become* Buddha. Hence the external entity would be "killed."

If a high proportion of people attain this level of maturity, society will of course be profoundly altered and perhaps itself will be considered to have matured.

We do not seek to mature as individuals in order to bring about a mature society. The mature society will be a pleasant and necessary by-product of widespread maturing, and its value lies in its providing a framework for easier attainment of maturity by the individual, and in the possibility of helping humanity to find a will and direction to which individuals can give allegiance.

The preceding pages have sought to define levels of maturity and the maturing process itself, to examine what limits, if any, there are to this potential (which every human being appears to possess), and to set forth a few practical steps anyone can try in order to realize some of this potential.

To deny a link between the reasoning mind and techniques of accomplishing higher levels of maturity would be as absurd as to return to the Victorian belief that reasoning power is all there is to the human psyche. The link between rational faculties and life's intuitive aspects is the same as the bridge between knowledge and insight. If this connection did not exist, then all communication, all education efforts would be futile.

The lists of attitudes and suggestions for getting leverage on self-motivation have been put forth in the hope that the reader, whatever his level of maturity, will find that attempts to move higher in the realization of his potential may surprise him by producing tangible and sometimes immediate results.

Every human tends to mature emotionally as time flows through his life. But most of the process is automatic, unconscious, indeterminate, and reactive. Very seldom is the rate of maturing what it might be if it were encouraged by a process of self-actualization—conscious effort and guidance. That this effort can be highly conscious without being self-conscious is shown in the strange nature of outwardness that characterizes self-actualization. Self seems best served and improved by looking away from self. Boris Pasternak, in his novel *Dr. Zhivago*, speaks of a locomotive whose headlight is mounted backward in an attempt to see itself. This is doubly futile, since it not only can't see itself, but it can't illuminate the track ahead, which it needs to do.

The expansive nature of outwardness in techniques of maturing suggests a potential of infinite scope. As individual organisms, we are each, obviously, limited: in time, size, power, and understanding. The process of maturing, even in the single individual, may not be shackled to such limitation.

There are more than hints of this, as we have seen, in

philosophies, religions, systems of psychology, and isolated examples of human behavior.

The admonition to seize on this possibility and to behave as though it were true holds a promise of escape from these limitations in ways undreamed of by most of us. Probably every human being senses, however dimly, however infrequently, properties of self-healing, kinship with others and the world, a vital hope of rescue from limitation. Our very suffering under limitations is evidence of something deep inside that yearns to be developed. If the price of developing it is the ego, it may prove a bargain.

Finally, "mature" and "immature" are not either-or propositions. They form a continuum that we can tackle a step at a time. There is a ladder out of the pit, a door in the dungeon.

If, having read this short, incomplete treatment of an immense, important subject, you are moved one step in the direction of further maturing, remember that the book didn't move you—you did it yourself, and there is nothing to stop you from going on from here.

# Selected Bibliography

Allport, Gordon W., *Pattern and Growth in Personality*. New York: Holt, Rinehart & Winston, 1961.

——, *The Individual and His Religion*. New York: The Macmillan Company, 1950.

——, *Personality: A Psychological Interpretation*. New York: Henry Holt and Company, 1937.

Barron, F., "Personal Soundness in University Graduate Students," *Publications in Personality Assessment and Research*, No. 1. Berkeley: University of California Press, 1954.

Bühler, Charlotte, "Maturation and Motivation," *Dialectica* 5, 1951.

Cabot, Richard, *What Men Live By*. Boston: Houghton Mifflin Company, 1914.

Cole, Luella, *Attaining Maturity*. New York: Farrar and Rinehart, 1944.

De Chardin, Teilhard, *Activation of Energy*. New York: Harcourt Brace Jovanovich, 1970.

De Ropp, Robert S., *The Master Game*. New York: Dell Publishing Co., 1968.

Dubos, René, *The Willed Future, Reason Awake*. New York: Columbia University Press, 1970.

Ellul, Jacques, *The Technological Society*. New York: Alfred A. Knopf, 1964.

Evans-Wentz, W. Y., *Tibetan Yoga and Secret Doctrine*. London: Oxford University Press, 1935.

Fletcher, Joseph, *Situation Ethics*. Philadelphia: Westminster Press, 1966.

Fromme, Allan, *The Ability to Love*. New York: Pocket Books, 1965.

Heath, Douglas, *Explorations of Maturity*. New York: Appleton-Century-Crofts, 1965.

Hutchins, Robert M., *Learning Society*, Britannica Perspectives Series. Chicago: Encyclopaedia Britannica, 1969.

James, William, *Great Books of the Western World*, "The Principles of Psychology," Vol. 53. Chicago: Encyclopaedia Britannica, 1952.

Maslow, A. H., *Motivation and Personality*. New York: Harper & Brothers, 1954.

Masters, William H. and Johnson, Virginia E., *Human Sexual Response*. Boston: Little, Brown and Company, 1966.

Menninger, Karl, *Man Against Himself*. New York: Harcourt, Brace & Company, 1938.

Overstreet, H. A., *The Mature Mind*. New York: W. W. Norton & Company, 1949.

Platt, John R., *The Step to Man*. New York: John Wiley & Sons, 1966.

Riesman, David, *The Lonely Crowd*. New Haven, Conn.: Yale University Press, 1950.

Russell, Bertrand, *The Conquest of Happiness*. New York: Liveright, 1971.

Silberman, Charles, *The Myth of Automation*. New York: Harper & Row, 1966.

Von Hartman, Eduard, *Philosophy of the Unconscious*. New York: Harcourt, Brace & Company, 1931.

# Index